Musical knowledge

Understanding and responding to music involves several layers of knowledge and insight: processes in which education has a crucial part to play.

The central concern of *Musical Knowledge* is the relationship between intuition and analysis as we engage with music. The dialectic is exposed on three levels: in considering music as a way of knowing; in the context of specific research into musical experience and music education; and as a productive tension in music teaching. This final part will be of direct practical help to teachers. Keith Swanwick suggests ways in which music education can be a vital transaction, giving examples across a range of music teaching – including school and college classrooms and instrumental studios. In addition to teachers, the book will be of interest to anyone who makes and responds to music.

Keith Swanwick is Professor of Music Education at the Institute of Education, University of London. He has been musically active throughout his career, notably as a conductor, and has taught at secondary, post-16 and university levels. He is the author of a number of books on music and music education, including *A Basis for Music Education* and *Music, Mind and Education*, both of which are published by Routledge.

Musical knowledge

Intuition, analysis and music education

Keith Swanwick

London and New York

First published 1994
by Routledge
11 New Fetter Lane, London EC4P 4EE

Simultaneously published in the USA and Canada
by Routledge
29 West 35th Street, New York, NY 10001

© 1994 Keith Swanwick

Typeset in Times by Michael Mepham, Frome, Somerset
Printed and bound in Great Britain by
Mackays of Chatham PLC, Chatham, Kent.

British Library Cataloguing in Publication Data
A catalogue record for this book is available from the British Library

Library of Congress Cataloging in Publication Data
Swanwick, Keith.
  Musical knowledge: intuition, analysis and music
  education/Keith Swanwick.
  p. cm.
  Includes bibliographical references and index.
  1. Music–Instruction and study. 2. Music–Psychology.
  3. Music–Philosophy and aesthetics. I. Title.
  MT1.S944   1994
  780'.7–dc20   93–24935
                                                                CIP

ISBN 0–415–10096–8 (hbk)
ISBN 0–415–10097–6 (pbk)

Contents

Illustrations

FIGURES

MUSIC EXAMPLES

Acknowledgements

I am deeply grateful for the stimulation and encouragement of colleagues, teachers and so many students over several years. They have sustained me at difficult times, kept me engaged in lively debate and opened new perspectives at every turn. The work of a number of my research students is discussed in the book and I hope they will not find it misrepresented. In particular, I wish to acknowledge the contributions of Dr Liane Hentschke who insisted that I clarify my position on the work of Piaget, my colleague Dr Lucy Green who read an early draft making very helpful comments and Dr Tom Regelski who gave me the benefit of his sharp and critical wisdom, attempting -- mainly unsuccessfully – to have me write American English. In spite of all this generous help, any slips and errors of judgement are my own but I hope that readers will find them expressed clearly.

I am indebted also to Peter Polfreman for preparing the music examples and to Nancy Williams who helped with the Index and other parts of the text. As always, my wife Maureen made it all possible.

Introduction

Introduction

To be candid, I myself, for example, have never said in my life a word to my pupils about the 'meaning' of music; if there is one, it does not need my explanations. On the other hand I have always made a great point of having my pupils count their eighths and sixteenths nicely. Whatever you become, teacher, scholar, or musician, have respect for the 'meaning', but do not imagine that it can be taught.

(Hermann Hesse, *The Glass Bead Game*, 1943, 1972: 116)

You may not like this music at first, but that is only because you need to acquire a taste for it, like a taste for dry sherry.
(A student teacher about to play Beethoven to a class of 11–12-year-old children in a tough inner London school).

In curiously different ways, both of these statements carry the same message: we only get to understand and like music by rubbing up against it. No amount of talk will get us into appreciating a dry wine. From this some may (erroneously) conclude that all talk of music and all music education that lies beyond the acquisition of skills – counting out the metrical divisions of beats and so on – is a waste of time, that musical knowledge is all down to a matter of taste, to experience, to inherited native wit or cultural environment. I disagree with this interpretation. Hesse is not here telling us all he knows about the nature of musical knowledge and meaning and the novice teacher has simply misread his students and needs to get to know more about the street culture of London children, which usually does not run either to lectures on Beethoven or dry sherry. There are layers of musical meaning, some beyond the reach of other forms of discourse and some much more accessible to talk, instruction, analysis. Hesse is more explicit about poetry.

I would also not try to tell them that poetry is one of the manifestations of the divine, but would endeavour to make the poetry accessible to them by imparting a precise knowledge of its linguistic and metrical strategies. The task of the teacher and scholar is to study means, cultivate tradition, and preserve the purity of methods, not to deal in incommunicable experiences....

(1943, 1972: 116)

Exactly; gaining understanding is a process of unwrapping layers of intuitively glimpsed meanings, exposing something (though never all) of the why and how of the objects of our attention. Throughout this book I shall argue that, though we certainly should have respect for the infolded and inexplicable 'meaning' of music, access to some part of musical 'meaning' can be gained and insights brought sensitively into the light of day without necessarily supposing it to be a manifestation 'of the divine'. Something of the 'meaning' of music can be taught or at least 'caught' from others. It can be learned. Music education depends upon the possibility of finding the equivalent of Hesse's 'linguistic and metrical strategies'; and this is rather more than the mechanical process of counting 'eighths and sixteenths', which might more economically and effectively be managed by a metronome or through micro-technology.

The first aim in writing this book is to try to tease out something of the nature and value of the strange activity we call music, to show why music can be considered to be a form of knowledge and how direct knowledge of music might best be facilitated. Musical encounters, though frequently powerful, are essentially abstract, difficult to pin down. Yet a large literature in aesthetics asserts that music contributes to the profusion of human knowledge, that it is vital for the well-being of human kind. It is not my intention systematically to review this literature, but to offer a particular perspective, following a method of enquiry which stays close to music itself and looks for an integration of theory and practice.

The working agenda for trying to understand the complex phenomenon of music can be neither simple nor procedurally pure. It is a project requiring an element of philosophical analysis but at the same time a willingness to get to grips with the untidiness of actual data; evidence as to how people (we) make and take music – an attitude that is empirical as well as reflective and which will not let us get away with unsupported speculation or poetic words about the mystical properties of music. We have to think imaginatively *and* observe carefully. At the outset then I declare a necessary impurity of method: this book will be both philosophically analytical and empirically scientific; it will also deal with the practical. Academically risky as this might appear to be, at least the approach to some extent resembles everyday life, where we simultaneously speculate, theorise and test out our hunches by experiment and observation. I believe this risk to be worth taking and that a truly cross-disciplinary approach is likely to be more conceptually illuminating and practically useful than the segregation of models and methods.

The reader should not therefore look for tidy encapsulated sections on this and that, but will find strands of argument which are developed throughout the text – more like the unfolding plot of a detective story than an alphabetically indexed professional manual. The method of working, though cross-disciplinary, is – I hope – disciplined.

It is obviously insufficient to study music by itself as if it were somehow independent of musically-knowing minds, nor can we simply report the working procedures of musicians, though these may indeed be important sources of evidence. To begin to understand how music works its spell requires us to think about how we perceive music; or perhaps better, how we *construe* it, what we make of it; or – to use a phrase suggested by Tom Regelski – how we are informed (in-formed). There is a vibrant relationship between music and human feeling that is not easily or glibly described and analysed. Yet it is important to attempt this analysis, especially for those who stand at the crossroads between music and people – musicians and teachers.

The two coordinates of this transaction are the nature and quality of musical knowledge itself and sensitivity in understanding other people as they respond to music as music-makers or music-takers in a cultural context. Music as a phenomenon, our response to music and the processes of music education are the three strands out of which this book is composed. The loom on which these elements are teased out and woven together is that of research, structured enquiry into music and music education. Three broad and related research questions are addressed philosophically and empirically.

1   What kind of worthwhile knowledge could be said to arise from musical experience and is there a deep structure to this knowledge that transcends local and historical differences of style and form?
2   Can we investigate response to music without destroying the quality of the engagement, perhaps trivialising it by an insensitive analysis, by inappropriate attempts at measurement or by inadequate assessment?
3   How can music learning and student assessment be best managed by teachers, and how might studios, schools and colleges become more appropriate places for activities that are in the richest sense of the term 'musical'?

The discerning reader will by now have spotted the tripartite shape of the book. The first part, *Musical knowledge and value*, is a conceptual exploration of the nature of musical knowledge, starting from a consideration of music itself rather than pre-arranged issues extant in the existing literature about musical knowledge. This takes us into the important role of musical analysis and concludes with a description of a small-scale experiment, the results of which seem to throw some light on the actual process of the acquisition of musical knowledge.

The second part, *Researching musical experience*, also begins with attention to music, initially seen from a composer's angle of analysis. This illustration of a composer researching his own processes leads us into a brief account of available research procedures, well-known investigative processes, many of which are subsequently to be enlisted to help us observe more carefully the unfolding of musical knowledge in the human mind. Rather than attempt any overview of research in the field, I have focused especially on the studies of some of my own students and contracted researchers working in my own department. Readers seeking a more comprehensive review of methods and problems in research are recommended to look elsewhere (especially in Colwell 1992).

The emergent view of musical knowledge and further implications of specific research findings are brought together in the final section, *Musical learning and musical teaching*. It is not my business to specify or prescribe detailed curriculum practice and day-to-day teaching methods for other people. Rather, I shall try to draw attention to those elements of educational transactions in music that appear to have the greatest vitality, and suggest ways in which they can be sustained, giving examples from a range of music teaching, including school classrooms and instrumental studios. It is this third part of the book that music teachers should find of most direct practical help, even though the roots of the ideas lie in the preceding two sections which – by exposing something of the nature of musical knowledge – may ultimately be the most useful.

There is a second main aim. A recurring theme has emerged in the process of writing and has become an important organising idea that links the three parts of the book and is an over-arching problem. Put bluntly, it is the dialectic of intuitive and analytical ways of making sense of the world. In Part I this issue is raised directly by consideration of music as a way of knowing. In Part II it surfaces as the apparent predicament between what are sometimes called qualitative and quantitative research paradigms. By Part III it re-appears as a dialectic tension throughout education – a pull between what I have elsewhere called encounter and instruction (Swanwick 1988). Here then is what could be called my 'formal theory'; 'rooted in many substantive areas', grounded in many data (Strauss 1987: 243).

Because I wish to avoid pitching camp exclusively with either intuitive or analytical thinking as though they were mutually exclusive, this book lies wide open to criticism by methodological purists. Musical analysts might doubt the level of rigour employed in dissecting pieces and those who prefer to talk in more holistic or philosophical ways about music will worry about the exposition of an analytical model which attempts to expose the dimensions of musical experience without reverting to the standard texts and following well-worn paths of argument. Empirical and experimental researchers may miss the detailed justification of methods and fully tabulated descriptions of findings couched in accepted 'scientific' research jargon. Those committed to a qualitative approach could find the element of 'top down' theorising distressing and will worry about experiments and observational schedules. Inevitably, these result in the use of graphs and tables to show group tendencies and the employment of statistics to sift out meaningful pattern from chance.[1] Empirical evidence by itself is not to be thought of as final and incontrovertible 'proof' but rather as illustrative of a thesis, a limited form of analysis, a cross-section of reality, a small facet of what is initially perceived directly and intuitively. I hope to show that direct and inarticulate intuitive knowledge underpins the building of all conceptual models and determines the shaping of experiments, observational techniques and interpretation of data. But left to itself, intuition is wayward and unreliable. We all profit from exposing data to the analytical light of day.

The music examples may cause some problems. For instance, the reader might ask why so much fuss is made at the outset about a piece of music by a turn-of-the century British composer. Certainly, American and Australian readers of an early draft of the text thought that this music would be unfamiliar to their colleagues and questioned the wisdom of its inclusion. My simple procedure has been to discuss pieces of music because they were in mind at the time and seemed worthwhile, not to get trapped in assumptions about representative 'masterpieces' or in maintaining some kind of equitable cultural distribution. To avoid both an implicit commitment to notated music in the western classical traditions and philosophical excursions into the differences between the printed page and an aural experience of music, I use the word 'performance' to mean either (a) the realisation of a composed and notated piece or (b) an improvised or completely aurally assembled composition or (c) the reproduction of music assembled on tape or computer. Throughout the book, consideration of some of these 'performances' returns into focus from time to time. Bringing back themes – both literally and metaphorically – from earlier passages is a structural feature of the book which may help to keep in mind the unity of knowledge while engaging in specific levels of analysis. For instance, having discussed the nature of musical knowledge with reference to a particular composition as a concrete example, the same work reappears later on in an empirical investigation of how children respond to it in the context of an experiment.

It is my hope that this book will be of interest to all who make or respond to music in any way; particularly to students of music and music education. Every musician is also a 'teacher' at one time or another and every effective teacher of music is inevitably a musician. Those who participate in music as audience are also on the 'inside' and may speculate about this strange and fascinating human activity. They might also find something to engage them here.

Although I have written with the benefit of much travel and professional interchange with colleagues internationally, it is important to acknowledge the British perspective. Way back in 1962 – as were many other teachers – I was working with children in school helping them to compose music in small groups. From a USA viewpoint, Bennett Reimer regrets that composing lags behind performance activities and sees the development of this aspect of the school curriculum as unfinished business (Reimer 1989: 213). In many other countries, especially in northern Europe, the composing strand of the music curriculum seems to be much more firmly in place; for instance, in Britain, close to 20 percent of school music time is spent in students composing. Composing – with or without notation – is a requirement for the public examination at the age of 16 (General Certificate of Secondary Education) and since 1992 composing has been an essential strand of the National Curriculum, legally required work in music for all children in state schools. Figure 1 shows the proportion of items that are listed in programmes of study that in 1992 became mandatory for all children aged 5 to 14.

Also characteristic of music in Britain is the richness of musical opportunities both in and out of schools and colleges. I count myself fortunate to have grown up in a vigorous and varied musical culture – directing and

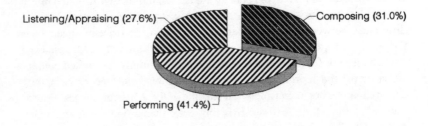

Listening/Appraising (27.6%)   Composing (31.0%)

Performing (41.4%)

Defined by the number of items in the Programmes of Study

Figure 1   Composing, performing and listening in the English National Curriculum

singing in church choirs, playing in brass bands, jazz, dance and symphony orchestras, conducting many of the standard works of the Western classical tradition, composing a little – and to have been an active participant in the development of music in the school and college curriculum in Britain and elsewhere. This beneficial musical, professional and academic climate – and especially my research students – has made possible the substance of this book. Other favourable conditions have been the personal warmth, commitment and professionalism of all those musician–teachers around the world whom I count as friends and colleagues, my students at the Institute of Education in London and the many professional and amateur musicians with whom I have frequently worked as singer, player, conductor and musical director. These people have inspired, often challenged and inevitably helped to shape the ideas which I try to express as clearly as I can in the pages that follow. I hope this will be helpful for someone, somewhere; at least to the extent that any text can offer some illumination into what ultimately has to be unspoken and can never adequately be written.

Part I
Musical knowledge and
value

1   The nature of musical knowledge

Without warning or preliminaries, *In the South* launches off into musical space. With a flourish and a striding fanfare figure over three simple chords – each in turn – triumphantly and with massive energy, the orchestra pushes forward and upward. Out of this explosion of sound the strings and upper wind float easily yet confidently downwards while a pulsing drum marks the time against a background texture of fanfares. The vigorous forward impulse is reasserted and the orchestral sonority is gathered into a single forced note which becomes the signal for the emergence of a broad curling melody against which the horns float their own tune, pushing gently yet firmly down. The fanfares surface again, stronger now than before with punched out notes on the brass erupting into a weight of sound hurled downwards. Strings step out with a square, firm marching tune while the lower brass edge up tightly beneath, insinuating a sense of pressure. The horns sing out exultantly until all breaks loose in impulsive flurries. The music begins to die away, themes become fragmented and all subsides into a single quiet note. The most striking features of the opening passage of this work are its vitality and exuberance. It reaches out confidently in sweeping emphatic gestures from the first phrases.

THE LAYERS OF MUSICAL KNOWLEDGE

Inadequate as any account in words may be, the passage above is how I might begin to describe the first two minutes or so of Edward Elgar's overture, *In the South*. The work was conceived on a visit to Italy and given its first performance in London in 1904, the full score published by Novello. In that year the *Manchester Guardian* newspaper critic noted that 'the new concert overture struck at once the note of joy of living in the midst of "blue Ionian weather"'. Setting aside any programmatic ideas deriving from the history and countryside of Italy, the opening is clearly characterised by tremendous weight, energy, outgoing and forward impulse.

Music Example 1
The start of Elgar's *In the South*

The work is not so well known outside Britain but is a favourite with those who make its acquaintance and especially with those fortunate enough to play it. Apart from any intrinsic value, its presence here is intended to give specific reality to an otherwise abstract problem: the nature of musical knowledge.

This is important. This chapter is a first stroll through the garden of musical knowing, without following a pre-ordained signposted route that is determined by received traditions of horticultural discourse or the technical labelling of flora and fauna. My intention just now is to intuitively savour the problem, not start in at once with pre-sets, prior controversies and 'isms' – the analytical 'defaults'. Some of these 'authoritative' voices will be heard later on – should they seem to have earned a place – but I am making no claim to be comprehensive or encyclopedic and I shall certainly not cite every text I happen to have read.

From the outset we ought to notice that drawing attention to certain features of music is inevitably a form of analysis. Analysis is by no means a dull or trivial occupation, diverting us from whole-hearted attention to music – though it can become so. It is simply a way of picking out patterns from an overall impression, for instance by focusing on such things as melodic development, harmony or instrumentation. These analytical patterns or cross-sections may (or may not) deepen our understanding of the work and they certainly have limitations. My own analysis above has the tone of voice and manner of a kind of narrative; it is a subjective impression, a description of the forward velocity and sonorous impact of the composition and is as valid in analytical terms as listing harmonic changes or modulations of key.

It is perfectly possible to approach the music from several quite different angles, for instance, as illustrating the working processes of the composer or from the perspective of the technique of orchestration. Any analytical slice is only a part of any cake; it is less than the total experience. But analysis does invite us to see the work from the inside; our overall impression may become modified by a new slant. Furthermore, in setting out my impression of this passage of music, there is a dimension of personal interpretation which may or may not coincide with any particular reader's response to the work. As Bernard Shaw says through the character of Undershaft in his play *Major Barbara*, 'You have learnt something. That always feels at first as if you had lost something.' Thus, we lose and gain by knowing more – by being confronted with a different perspective. Analysis not only reinforces what is already intuitively known but can also challenge the security that lies in existing knowledge, disturbing the comfort of the familiar, inviting us to reconstitute our perception.

At risk of disturbing those who regard music as beyond the reach of other than poetical words, my first foray is to map out an outline, an overview of musical knowledge – though starting from the intuitive reality of particular pieces. Can we even begin to understand what anyone might be hearing in this or any music and decide whether it is of any conceivable value to take the time and trouble to listen carefully? Is *In the South* or any music fundamentally a set of private experiences, incommunicable and varying from listener to listener depending on individual perceptions and responses, perhaps a sensory pleasure or an opportunity for a personal reverie but little more? This is an important question for those who work with music and especially for music educators. If musical experience were both private and transient – leaving behind in us no trace of its passing – it would be logically impossible to say that these encounters resulted in us gaining any kind of knowledge at all. Music might be thought only to temporarily distract us or to alter the mood of the moment. If this is so, then nothing of consequence is taken away when the music is over, no change of understanding, perspective or attitude, for some kind of change is implicit in any concept of 'knowledge'.

Knowledge is more than just undergoing experience. Even if we put on one side any idea of informational transmission, there is an implicit notion of enduring change; not necessarily a residue of facts but perhaps an unspoken change of disposition – an adjustment of mind or 'mind-set'. If music is to be thought of as entirely subjective and irrevocably private, then responsive teaching is unthinkable. We should forget education; those of us who can should just enjoy the fleeting pleasure we may happen to get out of music and let others make of it what they can. There would be little point in talking about it and no reason for trying to teach anything.

As an educator I am tempted not to take this view very seriously, and there are grounds for this. Of course, and to some extent, each person does indeed hear music somewhat differently, indeed uniquely. But response to music is not entirely exclusive to the individual, unshareable, idiosyncratic. If it were so then there would be little point in discussing, analysing or putting forward views about music and certainly no sense in making the study of music a compulsory element in schools and colleges or running courses of study – except to train performers to function in the same way that we might train dogs or doves. And we do tend to share a belief that there are mutual starting points for conversations about particular musical experiences, a possibility of connoisseurship or criticism. From an educational point of view, we do try to assess the development of students' musical understanding and therefore assume that not all of consequence is hidden from view and so inaccessible to interpersonal interaction.

Are we justified in making these assumptions? Look at our test case. Just as performers' interpretations of musical works can accommodate differing inflections of emphasis and musical judgement, so the interpretations of listeners may also vary. But there are limits beyond which we would have to say that people are not really comprehending the music that they may be playing or to which they might be listening. For instance, if the opening two minutes of *In the South* were to be described by someone as being emotionally constricted and generally pessimistic in character, made up of timid gestures and lacking variety, this might tell us something about the listener, but it says nothing about the music as conceived by the composer and understood within the traditions from which it springs and to which it contributes. Of course, the person might be finding it difficult to report experience within the limits of verbal explication – and there is certainly no requirement do so. But even making allowance for this – on the surface at least – there does seem to be 'objective' knowledge lurking here somewhere which can either be apprehended or 'mis-taken'.

What then is the form this knowledge takes, knowledge which we suspect may be gained through musical experience but find so hard to explicate? From the start we have to recognise that musical knowledge is multi-layered, it has several strands, often woven together in our actual experience though they are separable for the purpose of closer analysis and understanding. The most obvious and easily recognised category of knowledge is generally called 'propositional', informational, factual, knowing *that*. For example we may know that two plus seven makes nine or that Manchester is 200 miles from London or that *avoir* is the French verb corresponding with the English 'to have', that Beethoven wrote nine symphonies, or from where *samba*, *bangra*, *opera* or *rap* originated. It is a mistake to think that this is all there is to knowing and in the case of music this error is especially obvious and if perpetuated can cause educational distortion.

Imagine a young pianist struggling to play the *Sarabande* from the Bach D Minor suite in the *Anna Magdalena* book. As teachers we are obviously trying to impart more than just propositional knowledge, perhaps telling the student what a *Sarabande* is or on which instrument the piece might originally have been played. Such knowledge could indeed have an effect on the way the piece is played, perhaps helping to determine the speed that is chosen or whether or not to use the sustaining pedal or not, even suggesting levels of touch. If this were indeed so we could regard this as musically useful knowledge, in the sense that it informs our interpretation of the music.

Music Example 2
The start of *Sarabande in D Minor* by J. S. Bach (1725)

Notice though, that knowledge *about* things can so easily be acquired in non-musical ways. We could find out what a *Sarabande* is simply by being given a definition or by reading about it in a book and never actually play or listen to one, thus acquiring knowledge that may have some kind of historical value but is musically inert: second-hand knowledge. For this reason musicians and teachers have to be especially careful to relate factual or propositional knowledge – knowing 'that' – with other strands of musical knowledge. It is possible to have a precise knowledge *about* music but this is not the kind of knowledge that musicians and music lovers see as being crucially important. Edward Elgar once heard someone describe a phrase of Wagner's in terms of the chord of the supertonic. He responded with 'What *is* the supertonic? I never heard of it' (Shaw in Laurence 1981 III: 725). This is not to say that Elgar – though largely self-taught – was ignorant of the use and harmonic effect of supertonic chords, only that it had not been important for him to talk about them or label them in this particular propositional way. He already *knew* supertonic chords perfectly well as aural phenomena in the context of his own and other pieces.

This is an important distinction (to which I shall return) the difference between indirect propositional knowledge by description and that which is acquired and associated directly through musical experience. If the reader is unfamiliar with *In the South*, then my description is an inadequate substitute for the overture; if this work is already known then my account becomes an attempt to share and compare by analysis. In neither case can the music be replaced by the verbal description.

Gaining propositional information is obviously not the sum of musical experience and is certainly not the essence of musical knowledge. Although knowing music is clearly much more than knowing 'that', there is a danger that factual knowledge may be seen as central to musical knowing. Such knowledge is relatively uncomplicated to manage in classrooms, cheap to resource and reasonably easy to assess, and this is very seductive. The possibility of such knowledge becoming detached from a genuine musical context, learned verbally at one remove, at second hand – I shall argue – has always to be resisted. I therefore propose to concentrate not on knowing *about* music but rather on how knowledge *of* music is acquired, on *first-hand* or *personal* knowledge and its significance (Polanyi and Prosch 1975). In this exploration there are serviceable guides who have already mapped out some of the terrain, making useful distinctions between 'knowing that' and 'knowing how' (Ryle 1949) and between these and knowledge by 'acquaintance' (Russell 1912). A useful overview of these important distinctions can be found in Hamlyn (1970: 103–11). I shall try to articulate these concepts in the particular context of musical knowledge.

FIRST-HAND KNOWLEDGE

We might notice that our young pianist is intent on deciphering the notation: sorting out the chords, organising fingers. The ability to decode notation (or to write it) is certainly a musical skill which is of importance in some musical traditions, though by no means in all. There are also essential aural judgements to be made, deciding whether or not what is being played matches the notation, the ability to sort out, match, identify and classify the sound materials that are the basis of music. And most obvious to other people, there is also the facility to manage the instrument, to coordinate muscles and articulate keys in a dependable controlled way. I would put these various 'knowings' in this order of importance; aural discriminations, manipulative control and notational proficiency. Together they form a strand or layer of knowledge we can call 'knowing how', coming to grips with the *materials* of music. 'Knowing how' is a type of knowledge that we display in action every day. It is necessary for us to know *how* to do things, to operate a lathe, to spell a word, to translate a passage, to ride a bike or drive a car, to use a computer. Unlike propositional or factual knowledge, most knowing 'how' cannot be learned or displayed verbally, though workshop conversations and sensitive technical analysis can be helpful. Skills allow us to find our way into music but they can also divert us from further musical understanding if they become ends in themselves. We soon tire of empty 'virtuoso' performances. There are other important ingredients for musical nourishment.

The absolutely central core involved in knowing music can be appropriately called 'knowledge by acquaintance'. This particular way of putting it draws our attention to the kind of knowledge we have of a specific entity, something like knowing a person. For instance, we could say that we know Renoir's painting, *The Rowers' Lunch*, or know a particular friend, a student or a city. Knowing a person by acquaintance is very different from knowing things about a person. It is not just a question of being able to give their shoe size, height or weight – knowing that such and such is so. We might call acquaintance knowledge knowing 'this'; knowing *this* person, *this* place, *this* symphony, *this* song.

Acquaintance knowledge might to some very limited extent be demonstrated by propositional statements. If we are able to specify someone's size of shirt or waistline measurement the odds are that we might know the person pretty well, though not necessarily so. The sales-person working in a shoe shop soon gets to know my shoe size but may not get much further in knowing me as a person with all my 'thisness'. In addition, most acquaintance knowing is indeed likely to be tacit, unanalysed, unarticulated. We may not even have thought to catalogue the actual colour of our friend's eyes, let alone his shoe size, yet we undoubtedly have knowledge *of* that person and would – as we say – recognise him anywhere. Many writers on aesthetics have stressed acquaintance knowledge as being absolutely fundamental in the arts.

My dispositional knowledge of music is not merely general knowledge of fact, knowledge-that. It is concrete knowledge-of, of individuals, and added to in fresh experiences, occurrent experiences. There is *no* way of acquiring dispositional knowledge of music except by repeated occurrent experiences of it.

(Reid 1986: 46)

Some people would go so far as the philosopher of science, Michael Polanyi, in insisting that fundamentally '*all* knowing is personal knowing – participation through indwelling' (Polanyi and Prosch 1975: 44).

How then does this concrete 'knowledge of' music reveal itself in music-making? When our student is playing the Bach *Sarabande in D Minor* we might notice whether the choice of tempo, accentuation or articulation communicates a sense of expressiveness; not personal feelings in reaction to the music but a perception of what particular feeling qualities can be discovered by attending to the music itself. In a sense, these 'feelings' are objective, embodied in our experience of the music, arising from our interpretation of the musical object. For instance, does the pacing of a particular performance of this Bach piece give sufficient time for the dissonant chromatic chords to make their expressive point, yet not be so slow as to lose the forward flow that impels the melody and drives forward the throb of repeated bass notes? When we speak of expressive character we mean that a musical performance has about it a sense of individual expressive identity. This individuality may vary with different performers or for different audiences but in the case of a notated work any variation of interpretation will be within certain limits beyond which we would say that the character of the music has been lost, violated or perhaps transformed into something else altogether, as when Mozart is given a rock rhythm backing or a theme by Corelli is deconstructed by Michael Tippett in his *Fantasia* for strings.

But expressive characterisation is not the end of the story. A second element seems to be at work in the personal knowledge of music that overarches, complements and is fused with expressive playing, that of structural awareness. In Bach's D Minor *Sarabande*, we might look for a sense of relationship between the last three phrases of the first part, the final phrase being a lovely melodic extension in sequence with those that precede it. We might also notice whether the bass line of the second section is sufficiently clearly articulated to show its melodic relationship with the top line at the very beginning; really a virtually identical restatement in a different register, delighting us by the simultaneous existence of repetition and change. If these features of the performance were also evident, then it would suggest that the player had acquaintance knowledge of this particular work, knowledge going beyond both the necessary skills of 'knowing how' and even further into the music than the location and projection of expressive characterisation.

Music Example 3
The bass line at the start of the second part of Bach's *Sarabande in D Minor*

There is no need always to try to articulate such knowledge verbally; it is obviously present or absent in music-making and we can detect it intuitively by listening attentively. Here again though, it is possible to engage in helpful conversations about expression and structure and music lovers do it frequently. Analysis of these elements can be just as 'objective' as sorting out fingerings or bowing, in that they are open to view, embodied in the experience of the musical 'object' for those who know how to look for them. Although 'talking about' cannot be substituted for direct 'experience of', sensitive analysis can illuminate and deepen insight – but more on this later.

To complete this initial sketch map of musical knowledge we can recognise from our own experience a fourth strand, sometimes rather clinically called *attitudinal*, and characterised by Bloom and others as constituting the 'affective domain' (Bloom *et al.* 1964). We can respond to music with varying levels of commitment, or with none at all. One step up from an attitudinal bottom line of simply hating the stuff in general, might be when we tolerate only certain *kinds* of music, say romantic opera or heavy rock; or at the opposite far extreme, seek out opera or rock as a profoundly significant encounter, an experience that may become part of the very fibre of our lives. A spectrum of degrees of preference and commitment runs between these two extremes of negative and positive value attitudes. Musical valuing has roots in age, gender, social context, personality disposition and education, but most of all it depends upon the accumulation of previous musical experience. As a consequence, this knowledge of 'what's what' is deeply personal, highly subjective and varies not only between individuals but for any person over time, perhaps fluctuating from day to day. So at one moment I might feel that *In the South* is especially important for me, though in a week or so some other music may have taken its place.

The young pianist coming to know the D minor *Sarabande* may reach a certain level of controlled and musically insightful performance but may never come to feel that this piece is of value. To be more certain of the presence of a positive value attitude we would have to notice whether he or she ever plays it by choice, perhaps when alone and not asked to do so, or fishing it out some time later when other works are on the rehearsal schedule.

I am thinking here of experiential or direct valuing, when we as individuals find quality in an encounter. There is also the recognition of value at one remove when, for instance, I might say that although I cannot respond to some particular music, I recognise that it has value for others. Experiential valuing may arise from several sources; sometimes just from the sheer pleasure of manipulative control itself, or being taken with the way certain phrases speak expressively to our inner world of feeling, or the satisfaction of the structural organisation drawing the player into a perfect world of balance and completion. But the ultimate pinnacle is reached when these elements become fused together in moments of revelation, perhaps even having 'intimations of immortality', where the correspondence between the musical entity and our inner world is total.

> Imaginatively we stretch out towards what imagination cannot comprehend. We realise that there is more in what we see than meets or can ever meet the inner eye.
>
> (Warnock 1976: 58)

When we say we are moved by music, what is moving in us are the shadows of many previous experiences, perhaps forgotten in detail but unconsciously fused into a new perspective through the imaginative work of what we might call the 'inner ear'. These insights can be so profound that in the realisation of this deep strand of knowing we may be led to believe that music is so powerfully private and unique that it can never be spoken about, analysed or assessed. This is not so. The possibility of a profound sense of musical *value* exists only because of the development of sensitivity and skills with sound *materials* and the ability to identify *expression* and comprehend musical *form*. These strands of knowledge are neither completely subjective nor entirely concealed from view and we can find them at work whenever people talk clearly or write well about music as articulate connoisseurs, sensitive critics.[1]

We cannot say everything that we know of music but we can share some of our insights with others and it is certainly possible to develop analytical judgement, ways of describing and assessing musical experience which may deepen the understanding of the musician, the music educator and the music lover. A sensitive teacher or friend can help us hear what otherwise might have passed us by. Our capacity for knowing music can be developed.

RECURRING PATTERNS

If we examine analytical comments about musical performances, we shall find that they make reference to the directly experiential categories of *materials*, *expression*, *form*, and *value*. We shall also come across indirect propositional observations about social and historical context and other related 'facts', such as the construction and use of instruments. There are but a few ways in which we can talk meaningfully about particular experiences of music and these certainly go beyond technical descriptions and historical classifications. Here then are a few examples of critical comment taken at random from writers in various newspapers.

On John Harles, saxophonist:

> No one else creates a sound like this: apparently floating weightlessly, yet robust.

> The saxophone is a hybrid instrument – it doesn't have a basic sound of its own, like the clarinet....

On Des'ree, singer, songwriter:

> Melodies are simple and fluid. (Her) distinctive voice soars and sweeps impressively.

> ... there is something soothing and therapeutic about her music.

On Hole, rock group:

> ... negative emotions and abrasive noise.

On a performance of Brahm's violin concerto:

> ... it was a joy to hear the Violin Concerto in a performance at once so rich and secure... the glowing sounds...

> ... showed us a turbulent genius who deserved every brief lyrical respite the piece allowed him. Nor did he let the last two movements slip too easily out of titanic character.

> ... it was a genial giant who emerged, refreshed and lighter of heart, in the finale.

> ... culminating in a Passacaglia which knew exactly where it was going.

> Last week's spate of Brahms had taken on epidemic proportions by Sunday, but I would gladly catch the strain if one in ten performances were able, like Barenboim and Ashkenazy, to tell us what the fuss is really about.

On a performance of Verdi's opera *Un Ballo in Maschera*:

> This vocal overload even affects the orchestra, which is befuddled by the
> limitless tenor and can hardly produce the contrasts of expression required
> to bring out the psychological background to the opera.

These 'for-instances' confirm what has been already said about the ways we
think and talk about music, the strands or layers of musical knowledge. If we
are really attending carefully to music, we are bound to be aware of shifting
sonorities – the management of sounds, the secure control of instruments or
voices; the tone that is apparently floating weightlessly, yet robust, a distinctive voice, abrasive noise, the 'limitless tenor' who becomes a problem to
everyone else by emphasising control over his massive vocal materials at the
expense of the other musical dimensions. We are also conscious of the
expressive character of music – whether it is indeed a 'genial giant, with
titanic character', or lighter of heart, or communicating 'negative emotions'.
We also look for coherence, ways in which musical gestures evolve, relate,
contrast, find a sense of direction – the *Passacaglia* which 'knew exactly
where it was going'. In these comments we can also find the dimension of
personal valuing, of gratified commitment, embodied in such remarks as
'would gladly catch the strain if one in ten performances were able, like
Barenboim and Ashkenazy, to tell us what the fuss is really about' and that
'there is something soothing and therapeutic about her music'. Although
direct experience of music is always a fluid mix of all these elements, it is
possible to separate them out for the purposes of analysis. We have to
remember though that an analysis – though a potentially illuminating description of a cross-section of an experience – is not the experience itself.

Of course we can also comment non-analytically, propositionally, factu-
ally, on the context in which music is invented or performed. We might want
to talk about the social and historical background of music, how certain
instruments were made or played, observe that 'the saxophone is a hybrid
instrument', or gather information about the professional careers or the
personal life history of musicians, and so on. Interesting and valuable as this
might be, such propositional discourse can very easily arise without relevance to our direct response to music itself. Because of the potential
detachment of propositional knowledge, this knowledge strand falls into a
different logical class from the others. I will therefore concentrate on materials, expression, form and value and maintain that there is no critical comment
about any musical object or event – that is to say, any analysis – that does
not fall into one or other of these categories.

These dimensions of discourse about music are at the heart of musical
analysis and therefore of education and teaching, which is an activity essentially concerned with critical analysis at various levels and in different

circumstances, though often articulated in very practical ways. 'What would happen if we used a cymbal here instead of a gong?' 'What is it that makes that sound so brilliant?' 'Should this phrase flow quite so confidently forward or be more tentative?' Does that performance hold our attention?' These are examples of critical questions and some of them can be answered in practical ways, by musical experiment or demonstration.

But what of music in other than western cultures? Are we likely to find the same elements at work? In August 1989, I was privileged to visit New Zealand to take part in a national music educators' conference. Among the presentations was a session led by Syd Melbourne, a local Maori and student of Maori music. He took us through the elements of musical experience that he perceived to be important in the Maori traditions, in effect giving us a view of musical knowledge as he saw it within his cultural perspective. Throughout the presentation a pre-recorded tape of bird and other forest sounds ran on, as if to create indoors for us something of the environment of the outdoor world. The sequence of ideas as he presented them can be summarised like this:

> Music belongs to the world of Nature, of myths and stories and in the tradition we learned that 'sound heralds the arrival of knowledge'. Sounds heard in nature become imitated, reproduced, controlled by people. Seasons, tides and stars, the whole physical world seem to open up the possibilities of music. Then come the songs, those that tell the story of the unborn child – the struggle and the *haka*, a warlike song sung with strong emphasis by men. But there are also songs that seem to go beyond directly venting or eliciting feelings, the more controlled *waiata*, leading to traditional stories and sung by women.

> We then heard recordings of a flute playing melodies with regular phrases and sequences which also underwent variation and transformations. There were also songs by Melbourne himself composed in often fused styles – including rock music and Country and Western songs but still carrying something of a distinctive Maori feeling. He was clearly committed to music and because of this he had come to see himself as responsible for its transmission and development among the Maoris.

The order of this presentation seemed to me quite striking, for I had recently been involved in a study charting the musical development of children where we found the same sequence. In both settings, initial response to music seems to be an interaction with sound materials, delight in sonorities, noticing the calls of birds and sound of water which leads to the pleasure of controlling sounds, reproducing them, imitating birds or water on pipes,

Language

drums, voices. Out of these copies of natural sound grows the element of human expression.

Sounds are transformed into musical gestures and often related to dance; they may be suggestive of ideas, images, feelings; they can be transformed into warlike shouts, heroic declamations, lullabies, dances, stories. Shared meanings within musical conventions make possible communal participation and musical performances may become powerfully important sources of meaning at both an individual psychological level and particular traditions and cultures.

And these expressive ideas may be imaginatively re-configured or broken, perhaps by contrasting phrases, creating small embellishments, disrupting a rhythm, or in other ways playing with our expectations, our sense of musical future, surprising us. At this level music takes on organic form and seems to assume almost an independent life of its own, transcending local cultures and extending the range of personal feelings.

I find a parallel to this analysis of the layers of musical knowledge in the work of John Blacking, especially in his observations among the Venda people of South Africa.

> Often, when an infant started banging with some object, he or she was not told to shut up: an adult or older child would convert the spontaneous rhythm into intentional musical action by adding a second part in polyrhythm.
>
> (Blacking 1984: 46)

Here again we are aware of exploration of sound materials being transformed by skilled control, making it possible to fit in with others.

> As children grew up, they began to explore available musical instruments and tried to participate in performances. By the age of five or six, some had begun to learn certain solo instruments for pleasure and reflection, but all participated in the boys' and girls' play dances on moonlight nights, where they first learned to improvise words and dance steps, use additive rhythms, and lead songs – all good training for *malende* songs and dances, which were a major musical activity of adults (p. 49).

Dance, movement and story-telling in songs unwrap the expressive layer of music. And later:

> They had grasped the basic principles of harmony and could recognise two different melodies as transformations of a single harmonic frame-work; they understood the principles of repeated rhythmic patterns; and also appreciated that repeated melodic patterns could be transformed by the organising principles of tonality and mode (p. 49).

Expression is taken up into shared musical conventions and there are in Blacking's account glimpses of the playful possibilities of musical form at work in the transformation of phrases by transposition and modal shifts. Woven into all this is a layer of commitment and purpose, a sense of musical value, which Blacking perceived was being analysed by Venda people along the following lines:

> The aim of musical performance was to experience the spiritual foundations of the cosmos and the common humanity of every individual through the practice of music and dance (p. 44).

Materials, expression, form and value; we shall not escape these strands of knowledge whenever or wherever we think and talk about music. Such knowledge is surely more than a rather complicated way of gaining sensual pleasure. The interwoven layers of musical knowledge seem to arise – like language – in all cultures and appear to serve a need to make sense of the world, to celebrate life and living in symbolic forms. Any analysis of the so-called 'meaning' of music seems to be articulated within this matrix of *knowing*. As to music education: we may agree with Hesse that 'meaning' cannot be taught: a proposition at a fundamental level that is true of all educational endeavours. But we can *learn* to find meaning and teachers can facilitate or impede this learning.

To summarise: I have intuitively reflected upon musical knowing without much in the way of recourse to what may be called the scholarly literature. From this naive enquiry, musical knowledge appears to be either propositional or direct, by acquaintance. Acquaintance knowledge is prime, for there is no other way of accessing music, and it is complex, having several layers. These I categorise as materials (knowing how), expression and form (knowing this) and value (knowing what's what). Of these it is valuing that characterises the deepest levels of musical experience.

It is these strands that education in music may be supposed to develop and that process will involve analysis. Propositional knowledge – factual knowledge by itself – is very different from musical analysis, which is an activity starting and ending with direct musical experience, thus having the potential to enrich insights and enlarge musical response. But a great deal depends upon our conception of the relationship between analysis and intuitive ways of knowing. This is the main theme of the next chapter.

2 Intuition, analysis and symbolic forms

Music Example 4
A mystery piece, by Roger Bullivant

In failing to recognise [Example 4], the ordinary music lover may show himself to be more expert in harmony than he had imagined himself to be.

(Bullivant in Arnold 1983: 825)

THE CLAIMS OF INTUITIVE KNOWLEDGE

Intuitive, personal or acquaintance knowledge lies at the heart of musical experience; indeed, it can be shown to be crucial for all knowing. Its relationship to logical or analytical knowledge is something of a philosophical tease as well as an educational tension; there is a dynamic relationship between intuition and analysis which I have already hinted at but not yet explored. It is worth an excursion into this here – however briefly – for it may expose some misunderstandings that can waylay musicians, critics and teachers – indeed, any who think and write about music. As a starting point we should be grateful that a positive way of looking at the problem has been particularly clearly expounded by Benedetto Croce, writing from Naples at the turn of this century. The Italian philosopher puts his finger firmly on the crucial distinction and draws out some of the consequences. His forthright expression of this insight is proclaimed on the first page of his first chapter of the book, *Aesthetic*.

> Knowledge has two forms: it is either *intuitive* knowledge or *logical* knowledge; knowledge obtained through the *imagination* or knowledge obtained through the *intellect*; knowledge of the *individual* or knowledge of the *universal*; of *individual things* or of the *relations* between them: it is, in fact, productive either of *images* or of *concepts*.
>
> (Croce 1900: 1, italics in original)

He tells us that intuition reveals in a work of art not abstractions such as space and time, but 'character, individual physiognomy'. It 'gives us knowledge of things in their concreteness and individuality' (p. 5).

> Intuitions are: this river, this lake, this brook, this rain, this glass of water; the concept is: water, not this or that appearance and particular example of water, but water in general, in whatever time or place it be realised; the material of infinite intuitions, but of one single concept. (p. 22)

The sharpness of this initial analysis is welcome if somewhat polarised, an apparent dichotomy which can eventually be seen as dialectical – a relationship owing more to the idea of discourse than of dissonance. Croce does eventually develop these concepts in a more integrated manner but from his introductory analysis it is possible to summarise the two distinct categories in the following way. For the moment, this will be our starting point, though I shall eventually put forward a more articulated network of ideas which can be seen in dialectic tension from left to right.

Croce's forms of knowledge

Logical	*Intuitive*
Universal	Individual
Relationships	Individual things
Intellectual	Aesthetic
Concepts	Images

In identifying two forms of knowledge as Croce does, there is a premonition of what has since been affirmed in brain hemisphere research. In spite of a good deal of uncertainty about the functioning of the nervous system, it does seem that the left side of the brain tends to control the right side of the body and seems fairly preoccupied with rational logical analysis, the sequential, convergent and verbal; while the right side deals with the intuitive, the simultaneous, the divergent, the visual and the spacial. This poetical extract is by a student of Arthur Harvey, 'Cristy', and catches the spirit of the alleged logical/intuitive dichotomy (Harvey 1986).

The left	*And the right side*
succinct	*flowing freely, loose*
logical	*and lovely, charmingly*
practical	*unpractical*
step-ping	*secretly*
smart-ly	*sliding*
in-to	*into*

UNDERSTANDING

Whether or not there is such a clear physiological correlate with our psychological ways of knowing is not an issue here. In any case, setting out these 'forms' of knowledge as though they were opposed to each other can be misleading. As Christy imaginatively suggests, they are not really adversarial alternatives but interdependent and interwoven; together they lead to understanding. Should we persist with the dichotomy and go just one step further, mistakenly lining up intuitive knowledge with 'feeling' and link rational knowledge with the 'intellect', then we are likely also to fall into the error of thinking that musical responses and judgements are essentially subjective. David Best draws our attention to this unfortunate tendency, the belief that:

> the creation and appreciation of the arts is a matter of subjective feeling, in the sense of a 'direct' feeling, 'untainted' by cognition, understanding, rationality.

(Best 1989: 70)

Intuitive knowledge is not a form of day-dreaming but an active way of construing the world. It makes possible all other ways of knowing. It is present in mathematical and scientific knowledge as well as in the arts. We cannot know anything without an intuitive leap into personal meaning (Polanyi and Prosch 1975). Croce places intuitive or aesthetic knowledge at a more fundamental and prior level than conceptual or intellectual knowledge. In spite of the apparent polarisation which I have depicted in the table above, the two forms of knowledge are not symmetrically balanced by Croce but should be thought of as hierarchical in relationship (see Figure 2). Aesthetic knowledge can stand alone but conceptual knowledge depends upon a basis of intuitive knowledge. For example, if we are trying to address a problem 'scientifically', how do we know in the first place what the problem is and whether or not it is worth the effort? The answer is: by intuitive scanning.

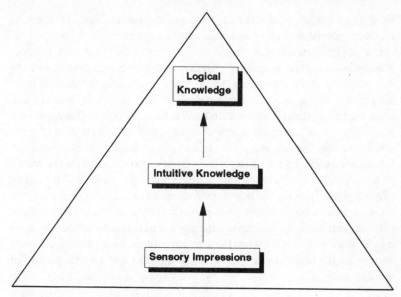

Figure 2 Croce's hierarchy of knowledge

Similarly, intuitive knowledge is not possible without our experience of what Croce calls the basic 'matter' of sensory impressions, the interface between the human organism and the world 'outside'. Sensory experience is not something to be left behind when intuitive knowledge takes charge. Nor does intuitive knowledge serve only as a preparation for logical thought, to be discarded when higher levels are reached. The relationship is not between contrasting functions but between previous and subsequent phases in coming to knowledge, in the same way that breathing starts long before we get round to writing poetry or scientific formulae. We cannot afford to dispense with breathing or eating just because we may want to get on with writing a book or setting up an experiment.

In a coincidentally similar map of knowing, the psychologist Bruner sees sensation, intuitive and analytical knowledge as three systems we have for representing reality, though he calls them by different names. There are some subtle differences in the angle of analytical slicing, but in certain respects the concepts are related: the *enactive* – where we know directly through the senses by actually doing things; the *iconic* – thinking in images, which enables us to hold in mind absent objects and events; the *symbolic* – where language and other rule-governed systems and conventions of thought extend the possibilities of abstract reflection and communication (Bruner 1972: 21).

Intuitive knowledge is essentially the exercise of *imagination*, the creative forming of images. And it is this iconic process that mediates between the chaos of sensory experience and intellectual comprehension. Without imaginative construction the play of light on the retina of the eye is a meaningless muddle, as indeed for some time after birth before we have developed ways of organising visual experience. Mary Warnock gives as an example of an imaginative act our perception of a melody, which we usually hear as much more than a bundle of separate sounds (Warnock 1976: 50). These tones are heard *together* as expressive gesture. To hear a melody as a series of separate notes is to miss the line and shape, though it is certainly possible to atomise it thus if we choose so to analyse, perhaps in a music aural test. The names of notes can be flagged up or written down but at the expense of the sweep of the melody. Imagination is at work if we are to sweep together the sensory fragments into whole phrases, perhaps as expressive gestures, enabling us to read musical meaning into sense data. Even a well-known melody by itself may be elusive to identify when taken out of context, as can be demonstrated by playing the musical examples given at the start and towards the end of this chapter.

> Without imagination, we could never apply concepts to sense experience. Whereas wholly sensory life would be without any regularity or organisation, a purely intellectual life would be without any real content.
>
> (Warnock 1976: 30)

The philosopher Kant also thought of the imagination as the power we have to form representative images, pictures, likenesses in the mind's eye (Warnock 1976). Similarly, Croce calls intuition 'a *productive* association (formative, constructive, distinguishing)' (1900: 7). His conception of the intuitive seems very close to that of Kant's idea of imagination in that 'it is the imagination which enables us to go beyond the bare data of sensation, and to bridge the gap between sensation and intelligible thought' (Warnock 1976: 34). And for Croce, intuition is similarly an act of representation, a *form*, created from 'the flux or wave of sensation' (1900: 11). And these forms or images are by no means only visual in character. Seashore catches the same idea in his discussion of the 'musical mind':

> Granting the presence of sensory capacities in adequate degree, success or failure in music depends upon the capacity for living in a tonal world through productive and reproductive imagination.
>
> Take out the image from the musical mind and you take out its very essence.
>
> (Seashore 1938: 5,6)

It therefore seems best for the moment to picture sensation, intuitive knowledge and what Croce calls logical knowledge as a cumulative continuum, with intuitive knowledge as the bridge between the others, a link made of dynamic forms, images, representations of many types. Intuitive knowledge is thus central to all knowledge, the medial exchange between sense and significance. There is nothing second-rate or substandard about knowledge that is fundamentally intuitive in character; it typifies most of our day-to-day realities, although by itself intuition has limitations – as I shall show later on. However, from here on I would prefer to substitute the term 'analytical' for 'logical'. This is a much less misleading word, since intuitive knowledge itself of necessity embodies certain processes of logical ordering, at least to the extent of a sequence of perceptual organisation and a sense of consequence or causality. Intuition may lead us in effect to say 'I feel that this is the right thing to do/way to go/answer to the problem'. There is at least the appearance of logic in our intuitive judgements – 'the heart has its reasons' – though they do not by themselves attempt to explain why, to analyse. And, of course, we can be intuitively wrong, bigoted, biased.

What then of analysis? Does it really force intuitive knowledge out, is holistic response inevitably left behind, in our particular case abandoned to the nit-picking detail of musicology, criticism, aesthetics or the psychology of music? Are we to agree with Nicholas Cook, that the music listener and the musical analyst – although apparently listening to the same performance – are really hearing two different pieces (Cook 1990)? Not necessarily. We must remember that analysis has two complementary definitions. On the one hand analysis is sometimes pulling things apart to find the separate elements, the component parts, what Polanyi calls 'subsidiary' awareness (Polanyi and Prosch 1975). On the other hand analysis identifies general principles that may link and underlie individual phenomena. This branch of analytical thought sustains many philosophers, especially those working in aesthetics.

So while a music critic may be picking at the details of a performance of *In the South*, a philosopher might be trying to understand the concept of performance and its relationship to a notated score. Are we then to imagine that sitting between them is the true listener, someone who is responding intuitively and holistically to the music without the handicap of the diverting clutter of analysis, neither listening for the balance between instrumental sections nor pondering the significance of aesthetic meaning? This would be to fall into the conceptual difficulties which Phaedrus describes in *Zen and the Art of Motorcycle Maintenance*. (For 'classical' we can read 'analytical' and for 'romantic', 'intuitive'.)

A classical understanding sees the world primarily as underlying form itself. A romantic understanding sees it primarily in terms of immediate appearance.

(Pirsig 1974: 66)

It is worth following Pirsig just a little further into his dichotomy, for – if we are not careful – it might also be ours, this apparent conflict of 'visions of reality' where the world is analysed dualistically into two hemispheres of representation.

The romantic mode is primarily inspirational, imaginative, creative, intuitive.

The classic mode, by contrast, proceeds by reason and by laws – which are themselves underlying forms of thought and behaviour. (p. 66)

To a romantic the classic mode 'often appears dull, awkward and ugly'. On the contrary, the romantic appears 'frivolous, irrational, erratic, untrustworthy, interested primarily in pleasure-seeking' (p. 67). This conceptual cleavage is unreliable and ultimately destructive – as Pirsig found. Intuitively we know it to be inadequate but find it very difficult to analyse where the fault may lie. The situation is made more difficult when talking about music because of the confusion between the aesthetic and the artistic which itself is a variation on the intuition versus analysis theme. Many of us have at times been drawn to the idea of the 'aesthetic' underlying the arts, a central, unifying concept. In *A Basis for Music Education* I made much of the term (Swanwick 1979), but I notice that it hardly appears in a later book – left out almost by accident – perhaps a subconscious conceptual shift from an unsatisfactory position (Swanwick 1988). We could just as easily place the 'aesthetic' opposite the arts in the models of knowledge that are initially proposed by both Croce and Pirsig. And this is indeed how I propose to argue: that intuitive or aesthetic awareness is a necessary but not sufficient condition for artistic understanding.

THE AESTHETIC AND THE ARTISTIC

In one sense Croce is surely right; what we call 'the aesthetic' is essentially our intuitive perception of the unique in the totality of its special context, it has to do with the particularity of experience. But it is a mistake to conflate the aesthetic with the artistic. Music partakes of the aesthetic attitude but for a composer or performer to make a musical work and for a listener to perceive it as being in some way significant requires elements of analysis. We are not simply shaped (in-formed) by music but actively attend to certain features of any performance, sorting out our own foreground from background. We interpret, construe, construct, sometimes in concentrated 'knowing' ways, sometimes intermittently, tangentially to other personal agendas. And we can locate the particular experience within stylistic or other systems of analysis.

The human mind can pass from the aesthetic to the logical, just because the former is a first step in respect to the latter. It can destroy expression, that is, the thought of the individual by thinking of the universal. It can gather up expressive facts into logical relations.

(Croce 1900: 35)

Though we are able to reflect analytically on musical experience, it is important to remember that encounters with music begin and end with hearing it 'together' and that intuitive knowledge depends as much on sensory data as analytical knowledge relies on intuitive shaping and selection. Though we need to have some ways of talking about music, conceptual discourse starts at the opposite end, away from the sensation of sound and intuitive images that we form in response to it.

Of course there is a danger that we may come to imagine that analytical knowledge is what music is all about and that teachers – driven by a curriculum specification – will tend to work analytically from and towards 'concepts', perhaps choosing music that exemplifies them. This can easily signal to students and any potential audience that a piece of music is merely an illustration of something else, such as the use of certain instruments, the conventions of an historical period or formal procedures and not a significant experience on its own account. Surely Beethoven did not write the first movement of the *Eroica Symphony* to illustrate the use of 'sonata form'. There is a risk of real and worthwhile musical knowledge eluding us if we choose to promote, rehearse or present music simply because it demonstrates some concept, perhaps that of minor tonality, or mixed metres, or opera, or folk song, or a modulation to the dominant.

To be able to rattle off 'first theme, second theme, closing theme' is a parlour trick not worth the trouble of acquiring. To have Beethoven's *Third Symphony* in one's blood and bones is a boon beyond compare: part of our rites of passage, a part of our tribal identity, an important part, it seems to me, of what makes us human.

(Kivy 1991)

The only justifiable reason for selecting any musical activity as part of an educational programme is that it has the potential of significant engagement at the intuitive level. Since formal education at the end of the twentieth century moves more and more towards left brain/right hand values, music and other arts teachers have special contributions to make to keep the intuitive alive. Writing from the discipline of psychology, Jerome Bruner sees a deadlock caused by the complexities of traditional analytical assumptions and procedures.

> Perhaps the moment is uniquely propitious for the left hand, for a left hand that might tempt the right to draw freshly again, as in art school when the task is to find a means of imparting new life to a hand that has become too stiff with technique, too far from the scanning eye.
>
> (Bruner 1962)

On the other hand (to extend the analogy a little), the ability to comprehend and follow the changing sonorous images that constitute our experience of music, requires more than what we might call an aesthetic attitude. There has to be a background of previous musical experience that permits the identification and discrimination of sonorous relationships, comprehension of the conventions of expressive character and an ability to bring to the encounter a sense of style and an understanding of the scale in which a musical piece functions, how it sets up a complex set of relationships and gets us speculating about what might happen next.

Symbolic forms develop within traditions of use, within conventions that give form to thought, making it both possible and shareable. These musical conventions are well-worked analytical frames, not the first intuitive stirrings. This is why it is important to move from the general term 'aesthetic' – that is, intuitive knowledge through sensory experience – to the 'artistic', in our case the musical.

There is always a certain pressure to surrender the analytical detail of musical processes and procedures – the artistic – to the intuitive glow of the 'aesthetic'. Sunsets, light on a wet roof, the smell of cut grass, the feel of silk, the smell of pizza, the sound of a brass band solo cornet in the park; these are or can be aesthetic if we choose to savour and contemplate them each as a unique, special, absorbing pleasure; taken almost directly through the senses. But every perception arises inevitably in the senses. What is different about aesthetic perceptions? They are moments of at-oneness; with nature, our environment, with other people. They usually happen without prediction and are not necessarily dependent on a reservoir of previous experiential knowledge. Of course, a sunset may remind us of the paintings of Turner or an ambiguous night sky of a particular painting by Magritte; if this is so then we are enriching the aesthetic with our knowledge of the artistic.

Our immediate intuitive response is given extra levels of significance by layers of previously acquired knowledge; not knowledge *about* but knowledge *of*. Aesthetic experience is usually an unlooked-for gift and the first sunset may be the most powerful sunset experience. Artistic rewards are earned by participation in traditions and learned by rubbing up against the artifacts. Unlike the freshness of the sunset, we have to work a little and this work is likely to involve coming to the work more than once and to include an element of analytical sifting as well as intuitive gathering. Thus, over time and with familiarity we come better to absorb and interpret the significance of what is before us. Otherwise art objects and events – whether well made or not – may pass us by. Above all, there has to be time and opportunity to come to know music by acquaintance, to relate to it, to find meaning in the experience.

There is more to art than the aesthetic; a thesis that is strongly argued by David Best (Best 1989). A fundamental difference, according to Best, is that an object of artistic interest has 'subject matter' (p.153). This is much easier to assert in the case of literature, drama and perhaps the visual arts, but in the case of music such a thesis is very much more difficult to sustain. In the search for subject matter, Best is driven to use the phrase 'expression of life issues', suggesting that in music 'meaning' and form are really indistinguishable, a view taken by Langer (Langer 1942). It might be better to say that 'meaning' can be identified throughout a piece of music but that it is always in flux and is not translatable. And the same should be said of literature. Does it really make any more sense to explain 'the meaning' of *King Lear* than it does to discuss 'the meaning' of the *Eroica* symphony? That music embodies knowledge is not in doubt, and although any 'meaning' cannot be fully described or transcribed, it can be at least hinted at, as I intend to show later.

The essential point is that it will not do to talk loosely of the aesthetic and it is unhelpful to insist that the word 'aesthetic' can be used interchangeably with 'artistic' and 'intrinsic' (Reimer 1989: xiii). Such semantic slippage leads to curious conceptual problems. Music has an aesthetic surface for sure – the sensory effect of sound. In this it is similar in kind to other aesthetic experience, say at a sunset or watching the rain bounce on a roof. This is just one part of artistic experience and it is not synonymous with art. The matter is further complicated by his use of the word 'art' to indicate a craft or skill – like golf or surgery, but in the context of 'music', 'art' means more than just a skill. Artistry in music is indeed in part a skilled endeavour, but it is also the creation and performance of something that is expressive and coherently structured in a sonorous medium. When Reimer says that artistic quality can be located in such actions as a golf stroke, he appears to be pointing to just the *skill* part of art, the use and control of materials (p.66). Curiously, as soon as we do this, the idea of the aesthetic seems to recede into the background. Surely it is better to think of the aesthetic in relation to its linguistic root – knowledge through the senses, the sensory basis from which skills and awareness of expression and form are put to work *artistically*.

When the artistic and aesthetic become so conflated it is not easy to grasp the affective role of musical structure. In discussing 'formalism', Reimer neglects a consideration of the powerful *felt* quality in response to musical form which goes well beyond what he calls 'using the mind to ferret out all possible tonal relationships' (p.25). It is very easy to fall into these polarisations of the intuitive and the analytical – the feelings and the mind – and to overlook the fact that form is initially apprehended intuitively and holistically. Grasping the significance of musical form is more like understanding a joke than knowing a fact, it is knowledge *of* in an understood context. One essential requirement of an artistic object or event is that something is not only expressed but that it is *well* expressed. This becomes obvious when we study children as they compose music. Sometimes their performances, though expressive, may wander about somewhat aimlessly. With increasing attention to compositional processes, the internal organisation becomes tighter and the various elements more integrated into a coherent unity. Leaving things out, putting things in, making things happen suddenly or gradually, causing events to occur at the same time or separately, contrasting or repeating ideas; these are all structural decisions.

Seeing the aesthetic and the artistic as overlapping but *not* as synonymous concepts gets us out of this kind of trouble. The aesthetic is initially present in any fundamental intuitive response to sound materials. The artistic takes this further into musical processes, as we empathise with expressive meaning and delight in coherent, lively forms; processes that transform and intensify aesthetic awareness.

> Our lives are formless, submerged in a hundred cross-currents. The arts are imaginative representations, hewn into artificial patterns; and these patterns, when jointly integrated with an important content, produce a meaning of distinctive quality.
>
> (Polanyi and Prosch 1975: 101)

This bringing together of chaos into order is what the imaginative act of image-making is all about. To come to a moment of integration, to a new apprehension, is often felt as release from the muddle of everyday life. As I. A. Richards depicts it:

> Everybody knows the feeling of freedom, of relief, of increased competence and sanity that follows any reading in which more than usual order and coherence has been given to our responses. We seem to feel that our command of life, our insight into it and our discrimination of its possibilities, is enhanced.
>
> (Richards 1960: 185)

All human thought is an 'imaginative representation', including scientific theories, philosophical positions and our mental representations of how we intend to get to our place of work from the station. The essential difference between thinking in the arts and in other symbolic forms is that consciousness of the process of creating meaning is deliberately extended, explored and celebrated; this intensifies experience, draws things together, giving us not the confusion of mere experience, but what Dewey calls 'an experience' (Dewey 1934; Regelski 1992). Because of high levels of sensuality, compelling expressiveness and imaginative structural playfulness, music is a significantly valued human activity, celebrated in every culture; it goes beyond the aesthetic, it is symbolic form, it is *made*, 'artificial'.

> These artificial patterns are, as we have seen, what isolates works of art from the shapeless flow of both personal existence and public life. They make of works of art something detached, in many cases portable and reproducible.
>
> (Polanyi and Prosch 1975: 101)

SYMBOLIC FORMS

It is essentially human to be at once an inheritor, part of a culture, and an innovator, creatively striving within or against tradition. How is it that we can step outside ourselves and our environment and at least appear to be able to contemplate the past, present and future, thinking not only about what we can actually see but also about what we saw yesterday, and – most remarkable of all – about what we have never seen and perhaps never will, perhaps the inhabitants of Jupiter or a unicorn. All this is possible because we are able to learn, share and develop systems of representation. These systems allow us to form images of the world – to imagine – and they rely on a two-way process. We can assimilate the world to our own perspective, interpreting it in accustomed ways; but we also accommodate to new realities, changing facets of the representational system itself. We can see this process at work in social interaction. Each of us is moulded to some extent by the society in which we find ourselves but we also shape that culture through our individual actions.

Representation of our immediate and remembered experience allows us to go beyond simply reacting, like a hungry penguin in the presence of a fish. Imagination creates a kind of space, a margin of manoeuvre, in which we can either absorb what is happening to us or re-shape ourselves to make sense of it; usually an element of both. We are able to internalise experience and reflect upon experience because we have access to symbolic forms; for instance, language, maths, art and music. This symbol-making facility enables us to become aware of and articulate dimensions of our personal history, elements of our culture, the perceived feelings and actions of other people, the movement of planets, the natural world around us. It also allows us to speculate, to predict, to make attempts to shape the future.

Symbol-making and symbol-taking are supreme human developments. The psychological space between one person and another, between an individual and the environment is mapped out through symbolic forms. The main criterion by which we assess the value of a work within a symbolic tradition has to do not with its social origin but with its cultural richness; are there levels of depth, the possibility of further exploration and development?

Music is one important and universally evident way in which people symbolically articulate their response to experience and thus are able to share their observations and insights with others. It has something, though not everything, in common with the other arts, in that it is particularly well adapted to illuminate those elements of human feeling which are fleeting and complex and universal aspirations which most people seem to share, whatever their culture. The expressive range of music is enhanced by its strong sense of temporality – like drama and dance – and is intensified by its abstract nature, the more powerfully suggestive by not being fixed to a set of designative meanings, thus allowing us great freedom of individual interpretation.

Initiation into symbolic modes is what education is about. We might find ourselves drawn incidentally into a tradition or specific subculture, or we may realise that we are developing as individuals; but these outcomes are by-products, just as happiness is a consequence of doing or thinking about something else. (Paradoxically, if happiness, self-development or cultural belonging become objects of attention they often seem to become instantly unavailable.)

The arts function powerfully as symbolic forms and musicians across the world have taken extraordinary trouble to make sustained, articulated performances that people respond to as though they were significant, meaningful. Musical value cannot be experienced without direct knowledge of music, engagement with the interactive elements of materials, expressive character and structure. Through these channels something is communicated, something is transmitted, some residue of 'meaning' is left with us. When a work of art stirs us it is more than simply sensory stimulation or some kind of emotional indulgence. We are gaining knowledge and expanding our experience. The same is true when we form music as composers or perform it for ourselves or others; at its best the act of shaping music is a purposeful attempt to articulate something meaningful. It need not be complex or profound, earth-shattering or of cosmic proportions but it will be articulate, expressive and structured and just as 'objective' as the spoken or written word, an equation or a map. There will at least be the potentiality of expanding our understanding, contributing to knowledge of ourselves and of the world.

Information about the world in the sense of factual knowledge is obviously not the 'content' of music. Unlike literature or poetry, music is non-verbal, lacking designative meaning or dictionary definitions. But music is not self-contained, hermetically sealed from everyday significance. It is analogous in many ways to the dynamic processes and appearances of events in the world beyond itself through its manifest weight, size and forward flow along with the manner of articulation – short, long, accented, and so on. As we shall see later on, performances of music have their own particular universe of gestures, of characterisation. Psychologically speaking, responding to musical expression is an act of accommodation where, to some extent, we become like the music, taking on traces of its dynamic feeling qualities. But there is also an assimilative aspect, where musical characterisation is transformed into a world of new relationships within the performance. Musicians – and music-listeners – imaginatively re-constitute possibilities by seeing new structural possibilities and come to 'new' ways of feeling. In this ebb and flow of expressive imitation and imaginative construction music demonstrates its kinship with other symbolic forms. Expressive characterisation and musical structure together lift music out of being a simple sensory pleasure and into the realm of discourse. And the idea of discourse takes us beyond intuitive apprehension. It has an analytical edge.

THE ROLE OF ANALYSIS

Intuitive knowledge is not dependable. Like a spring or river it sometimes gets silted up, requiring conscious attention, dredging, clearing the way for it to flow again, perhaps in a new direction. I take this to be the essential procedure of Freud and many psychotherapists, to attempt to bring to mind what lies out of sight, perhaps festering or at least disturbing, through the process of analysis. The necessity of going beyond the intuitive is evident in the development of symbolic forms. This has never been better expressed than by Bruner.

> Less demanding societies – less demanding intellectually – do not produce as much symbolic embedding and elaboration of first ways of looking and thinking. Whether one wishes to 'judge' these differences on some universal human scale as favouring an intellectually more evolved man is a matter of one's values, but however one judges, let it be clear that a decision not to aid the intellectual maturation of those who live in less technically developed societies cannot be premised on the careless claim that it makes little difference.
>
> (Bruner 1972: 67)

First ways of hearing – in our case an intuitive grasp of music – can also be extended, refined, enhanced. Like creativity, intuition favours a well-prepared mind. Without opportunities to engage in what Bruner calls 'symbolic embedding and elaboration of first ways of looking and thinking', intuitive apprehension tends to weaken and atrophy. Unsupported by any form of analysis to help focus attention and explore experience further, music easily becomes mere background to other symbolic transactions. At times this may be fine, but we should neither carelessly assume that music education makes no difference, nor too trustingly accept that it will. All depends on the *quality* of the transaction and the understanding that intuition and analysis are mutually interactive. Analytical conversations about music are no substitute for musical experience. As Nicholas Cook says, distinguishing musicological from aesthetic listening:

> ... listening to music for the purpose of establishing facts or formulating theories and listening to it for purposes of direct aesthetic gratification are two essentially different things.
>
> (Cook 1990: 152)

Indeed they are, but analysis lies at the heart of attempts to engage in education and feeds the imaginative workings of intuition with data, 'yielding more and more understanding' (Langer 1953: 105), informing intuitive knowledge though never replacing it. So teachers, students and music-lovers will necessarily become aware of music from what Nicholas Cook pictures as the weaver's side of the carpet: seeing something of the inner workings, the tied ends, the loose threads, the organisation of the colour scheme; analysing, cross-sectioning. This 'going behind the scenes' is necessary to give some kind of structure to any educational transaction, to organise classrooms, to get students going; above all to sharpen the perception of detail and alert us to aspects of the music so far unnoticed. Analysis is part of the quality of musical experience and nourishes intuitive insights. Put poetically:

> Quality *decreases* subjectivity. Quality takes you out of yourself, makes you more aware of the world around you.... Quality is not a *thing*. It is an *event*.... It is the event at which the subject becomes aware of the object.... Quality is the event at which awareness of both subjects and objects is made possible.
>
> (Pirsig 1974: 233)

Music is, or should be, an event at which quality is celebrated. It is more 'real', more vividly experienced and coherent than much of our existence. It saturates us in the aesthetic glow of sonorities but goes beyond, conveying expressive ideas in compelling if often abstract ways but at the same time – through its humanly created artistic structures – reminds us that these are, after all, only ideas and not some kind of fixed reality. We are invited to look at the world in this way or in that, as sensory data are gathered into expressive meaning and organised into coherent form.

In this way music-making – like all symbolic discourse – *is to some extent in itself analytical*; it is a process of selecting out 'component parts' – a cross-section of our experience – reconstituting them into new patterns that are governed by 'general principles', particular ways of construing what Langer calls the life of feeling. One side of musical experience consists of the intuitive or aesthetic savouring of sound, hearing 'as it is'; the other side is hearing – to use Pirsig's words – 'what it means', perceiving an underlying form; not of course the generalising abstractions of Rondo or Sonata form, but the ebb and flow of human sentience, the captured shapes of thought, of feeling. This is where the ultimate value of music lies. It is uncommon sense, a celebration of imagination and intellect interacting together in acts of sustained playfulness, a space where feeling is given form, where romantic and classical attitudes, intuition and analysis meet; valued knowledge indeed.

We can now draw together some of the key concepts that have emerged in this discussion, drawing together ideas from the work of Croce, Pirsig and others (Figure 3). These lists are not in any sense complete and the terms are by no means synonymous. But in so displaying them I hope to bring out

Figure 3 The dynamics of 'Quality'

something of the richness which makes their dialectic relationship so powerful. The space *between* them is where it all happens, where durable, sustained and evolving knowledge is engendered and shared; what Karl Popper calls 'World Three' (Popper 1972) and Pirsig calls 'Quality'. We are here concerned with symbolic forms, communally significant objects and events, productive, meaningful discourse.

From here on I shall place the intuitive side on the left of the page to signify that this mode of knowledge is always chronologically *a priori*. It is also the holistic condition to which knowledge returns after the work of analysis. (The terms 'romantic' and 'classical' have here the meanings given by Robert Pirsig, the rest mostly belong to Croce.)

Music Example 5
The start of Henry Mancini's *Moon River* (Arnold 1983: 824)

We recognise *Moon River* in a holistic intuitive act, not by isolating the melody but apprehending it through its melodic/harmonic totality, as can easily be seen by comparison with the music excerpt at the beginning of this chapter, which – though theoretically the same melody – is in practice very hard to identify. In essence, intuitive knowledge is the bridge of imagination between sensation and analysis. It is pre-analytical. But left to itself, untended, not taken up into symbolic forms, intuition cannot thrive. As soon as intuitive insight is shared with other people as symbolic form it is inevitably drawn into the analytical processes of sifting, selecting, filtering and reconstitution. A work of art itself partakes to some degree of analysis; it is an event in which are joined aesthetic response and articulated discourse within traditions of shared meanings, in what Peter Abbs calls a symbolic order.

> If we accept the idea of a common symbolic order, if we accept the idea of a discipline having a body of distinctive works, and a range of conventions, if furthermore, we accept that creative powers and aesthetic appreciation develops in continuous contact with the whole field of the

art form, then it follows that one of the art-teacher's major tasks is to take the student into the 'cosmos of art'.

(Abbs 1989: 11)

Entering into symbolic discourse is both more and less than what is sometimes called 'the aesthetic'. Through a matrix of images, metaphors and other conventions of shared meaning, participation in an art object or event pushes us beyond the merely intuitive towards analytical frames of reference – seeing or hearing in this way or in that. Learning can indeed feel like loss, as intuition is probed and stretched, as different facets or components of the experience are probed, as ideas are traced through into new formulations. In this way music generates new knowledge; we come to see things differently as intuitive understanding is re-defined.

> When analytic thought, the knife, is applied to experience, something is always killed in the process. That is fairly well understood, at least in the arts. – But what is less noticed in the arts – something is always created too. And instead of just dwelling on what is killed it's important also to see what's created and to see the process as a kind of death–birth continuity that is neither good nor bad, but just *is*.

(Pirsig 1974: 77)

We are now able to distinguish two forms of analysis specifically in relation to music. *Primary* or intrinsic analysis exists as an essential element of musical comprehension, a symbol-making and symbol-sharing activity involving the processes of selection, interpretation and reconstitution of intuitive data. *Secondary* or extrinsic analysis consists of reflective discourse about particular music – the more usually understood definition. To this end, various forms of notation and other iconography may be pressed into service; words, physical movement, drawing and other metaphorical representations may all serve analytical purposes. Primary analysis is wordlessly implicit in all musical experience; secondary analysis involves extra-musical ways of pointing to these insights.

We need to distinguish both of these processes of analysis from gathering propositional information about the context of music; knowledge which may include facts about historical and sociological backgrounds or classification by genre and form, but by itself, takes us no further into music. Propositional knowledge enters the dynamic process of musical knowing when it provides a vocabulary and a framework for secondary analysis. If the parameters of musical knowledge are adequately represented, then secondary analysis – the usual meaning of the term 'analysis' – is an activity which can enlarge rather than constrain intuitive response. Unnecessary in our private dealings with music, it lies at the heart of music education, an endeavour which presupposes an exchange of perspectives.

Useful as this conceptual ground-clearing might be, it is time now to move towards empirical work, taking with us what we are finding in the philosopher's armchair and testing it out through more structured observations of how people engage with music. The parameters encompassing analysis have already been sketched out in the previous chapter and I shall return to them later. Meanwhile, the first practical step will be to see what can be learned from a small and unambitious experiment, in which children are asked to engage in a simple form of secondary analysis – encouraged to describe a piece of music in ways that could conceivably represent the essential knowledge layers: materials, expression, form and value. We shall also see what tends to happen when those responsible for planning music education try to proceed without an adequate epistemological map.

3   Musical knowledge in action

A colleague – a member of a prestigious choir – described his changing
relationship with a large-scale choral work over several weeks of rehearsal.
At the early sessions he found the piece fairly tedious and uneventful, heavy
going and lacking in significance, except for a couple of moments here and
there. The experience was, he said, a bit like travelling through an arid desert,
now and then coming across an occasional oasis of interest. But as rehearsals
passed and with growing familiarity, more watering places were discovered,
more pages contained moments of interest and significance. By the time of
the performance the desert had become a lake. His first intuitive response
had been superseded – informed – by further acquaintance and analysis – for
in music rehearsals a good deal of detailed analysis is bound to take place,
including attention to expressive detail, practising passages in different ways,
singing, playing and listening to parts in isolation, and so on. A growing
knowledge of the work from the inside had given him new perspectives. The
Sahara had receded.

His involvement was essentially practical but we might fairly confidently
assume that a similar process occurs when we 'take' rather than 'make'
music. As with performers so with audience-listeners; getting to know music
is essentially acquaintance knowledge, though on acquaintance we may
decide not to engage further. There are some important practical consequences here, especially for those involved in education at any level. It is
hard to imagine that we would play a piece just once, unless it is extremely
easy, but as listeners we often hear performances or overhear only a part of
performances for the first and last time. This can happen especially with radio
broadcasts but also occurs in educational settings, for instance, where we are
asked to sample a performance as an illustration of something else – perhaps
as an example of a historical period or genre. There might even be a negative
effect should the idea be put into our minds that this is really what listening
to music is all about – the acquisition of contextual information. Now I want
to test out the validity of the theory of acquaintance-knowledge in two quite

different practical realities: under the more objective scrutiny of empirical research and in the highly politicised arena of schooling and curriculum design.

SETTING UP AN EXPERIMENT   *'Listening + Appraising'*

An experiment in this sensitive area need not be a paltry or inconsequential exercise, provided that the assumptions behind it are musically valid. For musicians and teachers it is of some importance to know whether and how to organise audience-listening and to find out – not simply presume – if the reported experience of my colleague with the choral piece has qualities in common with a listening audience, including those students in school and college. Given a potentially rich musical experience, might they share his sense of a receding desert and growing pools of water?

Before setting off to gather data of any kind we need possession of a map, in this case a theory of musical knowledge to guide us, however provisional and roughly drafted. Fortunately I happen to have one, though so far I have presented it only as an outline, a sketch, consisting of a description of the layers of musical perception and response. These identifiable strands of musical experience constitute in our minds its essential fabric, each of which can be a focus for analysis: materials, expression, form and value. Although intuitive knowledge of music may comprise a response in all four layers fused together simultaneously, they can be separated out for the purpose of analysis.   *dimensions of musical knowledge*

The main hypothesis is that musical knowledge is essentially acquaintance knowledge – knowledge *of*. We might therefore predict that repeated exposure to the same piece of music is likely to increase our knowledge of it, even if no further information is given. With the dimensions of musical knowledge in mind, we might also be more specific in predicting that – given repeated opportunities to listen – a musical performance will come to be heard differently, perhaps as more clearly expressive and possibly more or less varied and complex. There may also be changes in our impressions of sound quality, perhaps in terms of brilliance and thickness (materials) and possibly certain modifications in value attitudes, perhaps perceiving hearing the music as more of a good than a bad experience, more oasis than desert or indeed, the reverse. Familiarity can breed contempt as well as foster positive insights. However, the main aim of this experiment is not to ascertain levels of preference, 'taste', or liking. That is a well-trodden road (for example, Bartlett 1973, Bradley 1971, Wapnick 1976, Sluckin *et al.* 1982 and Hargreaves 1984). Just now I am interested not so much in how music is received but how it is perceived.

We have an awkward experimental problem at the outset. As John Sloboda reminds us, it is very difficult to get into the mind of a music-listener.

> The principal problem facing the student of listening processes is to find a valid way of tapping the moment-to-moment history of mental involvement with the music.

(Sloboda 1985)

For a listener to give any kind of account of what is going on in music is to divert attention to some extent from the music itself, to move away from the direct intuitive experience of music to secondary or extrinsic analysis. Asking for a response in words is certainly problematic, relying on linguistic abilities which may not always adequately reveal levels of musical discernment and richness of response. In an effort to catch glimpses of the 'moment-to-moment history of mental involvement' it is tempting to ask for a continuous verbal commentary, perhaps recorded (Bartlett 1973). The diversionary effect of this 'talking through' may be quite powerful and other methods can be equally problematic and may lead to trivial or peripheral accounts of the music.

Devising a way of gathering responses to music is always crucial and it is necessary here to give some detail. It was decided to utilise the semantic differential, a well-tried if somewhat blunt instrument consisting of adjectival opposites.[1] A version was constructed which would at least have the possibility that some scales might pick up response to particular musical elements, those of materials, expressive character and structure. In effect, the semantic form is an instrument of musical analysis. It may not tell us much about 'the moment-to-moment history of mental involvement with the music' but it might reveal something about how a relationship with a musical work is built up over time.

ACTIVE	——:——:——:——:——:——	PASSIVE
VARIED	——:——:——:——:——:——	ALL THE SAME
DARK	——:——:——:——:——:——	BRIGHT
SMALL	——:——:——:——:——:——	LARGE
GOOD	——:——:——:——:——:——	BAD
SIMPLE	——:——:——:——:——:——	COMPLEX
THICK	——:——:——:——:——:——	THIN

There is one potentially evaluative scale, Good/bad, and here we need to make a distinction. Value judgements appear to take place on two levels. It is one thing to accept or reject a musical performance on the basis of direct and sustained acquaintance, with a real understanding of the significance of the layers of materials, expressiveness and form. But it is a very different matter to dismiss any music out of hand without ever attending to it, perhaps on the basis of peer-group solidarity or social status. 'Good/bad' is an ambiguous scale which may be used to signal instant prejudice or to denote an attitudinal outcome of critical awareness – appreciative or otherwise.

These semantic scales were chosen with some care and evaluated positively beforehand by five independent people. The seven scales are not taken 'out of the air' but are credibly related to the musical knowledge layers of materials, expression, form and value. The rate and change of onward movement is a prominent feature of musical expression and the scale Active/passive is a likely candidate for characterising the degree of forward propulsion. Large/small has obvious potential for describing the perceived weight of a musical gesture, perhaps communicated through accentuation, loudness or register; though it might also be descriptive of sound materials, an impression of the instruments or ensemble.

Thick/thin and Dark/bright are attempts to pick up perceptions of tonal colour, or sonorities, though these words could also be expressive descriptions. Musical form is likely to be represented to some extent by the scales Simple/complex and Varied/all-the-same. Musical value might be picked up by the Good/bad scale, although this could also signify a general prejudice for or against the music on the basis of identifying its cultural origins and counting it in or out of our accepted range. We do this all the time, changing the pre-set buttons on the radio should we accidentally find ourselves on the 'wrong' channel.

Although these scales may be interpreted by people in different ways, these interpretations are unlikely to alter radically for any *individual* in a short space of time. The experimental design is that of repeated measures; the same children were to have *three* opportunities to respond to the same piece of music at weekly intervals – the same time in each lesson – and any change on the scales can be charted for each child. The age of the children was to be between 12 and 13, old enough to be able to cope easily with the level of analysis required with the check form.

The procedure is simple: subjects listen to music and afterwards mark one of the seven spaces between the two extremes on every scale. The 'positive' and 'negative' ends of scales are switched around to prevent automatic scoring down one side or the other and to help focus on making a judgement for each separate scale. Despite obvious limitations – particularly that of making a static once-for-all description of a mobile event – there are certain advantages with this device. Although words are employed to generate the sematic opposites, a response in words is not required. Thus verbal fluency is not being assessed and no potentially distracting verbal account takes place

at any time, certainly not during the musical performance.

The chosen music has to meet certain criteria: firstly, of being in an idiom not perceived as exotic or strange; secondly, of itself being unfamiliar; thirdly, it has to be clearly expressively characterised while being complex enough for people to discover new aspects on subsequent hearings, though not excessively changeable – for that would make a snapshot type of description on semantic scales very difficult, probably impossible. This is where the first two minutes of Elgar's *In the South* re-enters the arena. This major paragraph of the concert overture has about it a sense of musical wholeness; many major ideas have been revealed and a structural turning point is reached when we can quite legitimately stop and ask, 'what about that?'. It is a place where Elgar himself took a deep breath before moving on.

Three London secondary school music teachers offered to help with this experiment and each identified an average to 'bright' class with a regular music lesson at weekly intervals.[2] Seventy-one young people (12–13 years old) from three schools were present at all three weekly sessions and each was allotted a personal number to preserve anonymity while keeping track of who was who over time. A blank copy of the form was given to each student for each session. There was to be no discussion about the music. A couple of practice runs were made at the start of the first session, for example, using the semantic scales to describe 'an angry elephant'.

INTERPRETING THE FINDINGS

The initial analysis indicated that the first two minutes of *In the South* were mostly perceived from the very first hearing as on the side of active, varied, dark, large and complex. By the third session, most of the students were hearing the music as generally more active, though the other scales showed little consensus of any kind. However, on inspection of these data it became clear that at the very first session many of the children were using the extreme limits of scales to describe the music – mostly the 'positive' end. This obviously removes the possibility of going any further in that direction on subsequent hearings. If on first acquaintance we describe something as being active in the extreme it becomes impossible to be more emphatic in rating on subsequent occasions; we shall have used up the ace card. I decided to examine separately those scores on the first hearing which ranged from 0–4 and those spanning 4–7. This division of responses into first-time 'low' and 'high' produced clear patterns of significant change over the three sessions. Figure 4 shows average changes over the three hearings when first scores were at the lower end of the scales.[3] In the interests of analytical clarity, the values of the scales Active/passive, Varied/all-the-same, Good/bad and Thick/thin are reversed to identify 'positive' ends of scales always with larger numbers.

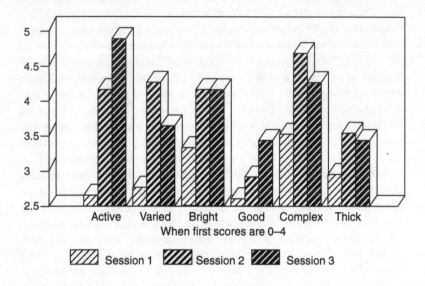

Figure 4   Responses to *In the South* over three sessions

The next move was to examine more closely the response of those children who at first gave descriptions at the high end of scales. Only two scales – 'bright' and 'good' – produce statistically significant changes after first time 'high' scores.[4] Figures 5 and 6 show the number of students whose assessments became either more positive or more negative on second and third hearings. 'Low' and 'high' first scores are both shown and zero level is the first score base-line.

The scores of those who started with high 'bright' and high 'good' perceptions tend to move in the opposite direction to those whose first description was at the lower end of the two scales. There may be an explanation for this which we shall consider shortly.

Even this modest and unsophisticated experiment demonstrates something of the complexity of evaluating the experience of audience-listeners. The description of a piece of music in such general terms is always problematic. After all, music changes as it moves along and perceived levels of 'activity' or 'size' will vary, depending on what is perceived to be happening from moment to moment. However, many performances have a general expressive charge – perhaps delicate or restrained, like a lullaby, massive and strident, march-like. Although such descriptions are of necessity metaphorical,

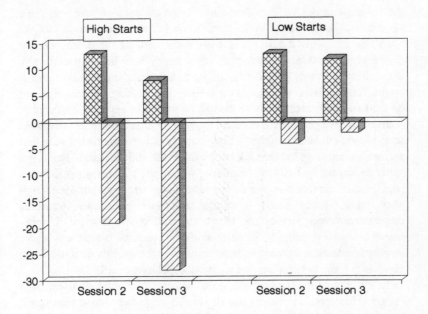

Figure 5 'Bright' – direction of movement for all students from the first session

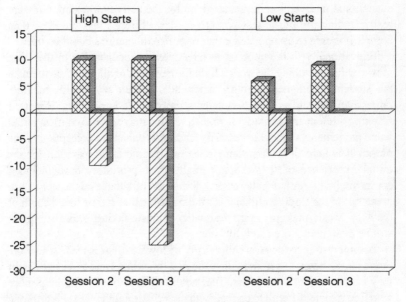

Figure 6 'Good' – direction of movement for all students from the first session

the semantic scales yield evidence of a large measure of inter-subjective agreement, changes in the same direction on further acquaintance with the music. In the case of the first time low-scorers there are significant positive changes over the three sessions on all seven scales. With growing familiarity these children mostly perceive the music as becoming more active, varied, bright, large, good, complex and thick. The most striking changes of all are on the two scales most likely to describe elements of expressive character, 'active' and 'large'. Here a constant upward trend is clear. The 'structure' scales – 'varied' and 'complex' – both show a positive increase between first and second hearings but then fall back a little at the third session. This is not really so surprising. Growing familiarity with music may permit us to hear a performance as more complex and varied than on first acquaintance, though after a while we may cease to be so impressed by deviations and contrasts as they become more predictable. This is the well-known inverted 'U' phenomenon, very commonly found in studies of musical preference, where levels of preference increase on familiarity and subsequently diminish when familiarity turns to boredom (see for instance, Hargreaves 1984).

In the case of the 'bright' and 'good' scales, those children giving high ratings at first tended to move – if at all – in a negative direction on subsequent hearings. This might be accounted for by them having nowhere else to go in a positive direction – such are the limitations of a seven-point scale. Alternatively it may be that by a third hearing, embarked upon without any educational intervention or reason given for the activity, the children were really finding the music less attractive – less 'bright', less 'good' – than before. It is safe to assume that either or both explanations could be true.

Educationally, it is important to have reasons for listening to the same music again, searching the work a little further. Best of all would be to relate the students' audience-listening experience to their own music-making, rather than separate it out as an isolated activity – as 'appreciation'. Repeated listening without any preparation or intervention may serve to confirm initial value judgements without necessarily leading to enhanced perception of the music. It is here that classroom strategies are crucial. Preparation for the initial experience of *In the South* might more profitably have included composing with fanfare patterns or a discussion of what it might feel like to break out of the English climate into the sunshine that can be found south of the Alps. Music-making can lift the quality of music-taking. This assumption will be examined more carefully later.

It is interesting to focus on children giving lower ratings at the first session. Some people seem to get into things the first time round and to a large extent they can look after themselves. Teachers need to know how to help those who find it more difficult to engage with music. Although there was minimal educational intervention here, it did appear to have positive outcomes for several possible reasons. First, they were asked to listen more than once to give intuitive acquaintance knowledge a chance. Second, the semantic form invited them to analyse the music along certain parameters, to pay closer attention, to engage with it and exercise critical judgement. And this they mostly did.

There is of course the ambiguity about the 'Good/bad' scale. This might pick up something of value attitudes towards *In the South* or simply detect prejudice towards the idiom and its cultural context. Is the music of Elgar an automatic 'turn-off' for many children of this or any age? This may be so, although his name is now listed in the English National Curriculum. It is perfectly possible to recognise the tremendous activity and weight, the complexity and variety of this music and at the same time not rate it very highly within our own personal value framework. Even those children who tended to move towards 'good' on the second and third sessions rarely gave the highest scores, and the average by the third hearing is still below the median score of four. The music may have meaning 'to' children of this age but not much meaning 'for' them, in that though they perceive something of its character and structure, it still leaves them comparatively cold and is not felt to relate strongly and positively to their value systems (Swanwick 1979).[5]

It is clear that one condition for the development of musical knowledge is repeated opportunities to cultivate a *relationship*. This relationship thrives on insightful preparation, models of musical commitment and the possibility of making associations between lively musical traditions in the world at large and music-making in the classroom. Through composing and performing, repeated exposure is inevitable. If audience-listening is to be a part of any music curriculum, then ways have to be found of sustaining these encounters in a meaningful way. Above all, the music must be given a chance to speak for itself.

When a person attends responsively to the first two minutes of *In the South*, he or she is sharing intuitively a perspective on human feeling and enjoying a period of freedom from verbal discourse and the unsatisfactory consequences of the fragmentation that pervades most of our lives. A sense of massive energy composed of shining, hard, large yet fluid sounds bounds forward into open space and floats forward. Throughout there is much coming and going of ideas weaving together and apart, all different yet related to each other. To call it massively optimistic is a simplistic distortion but perhaps something like that is not entirely out of place? As an image of human feeling it certainly offers us a distinctive perspective. No propositional knowledge about the composer, his life and times or his cultural values can replace this, though should we find such an experience significant we shall almost certainly want to know more about its context and origins.

This drawing together of unspoken things as we relate to a unique unified artistic object is not an escape from life in general or from the effort of logical thinking. Rather it is a lively way of opening up new avenues of perception, contemplating possibilities of intuitive knowledge other than those we habitually espouse and enriching our understanding by renewing in us a sense of wholeness, integrity. Such an experience, this knowledge of music, leaves a residue of impressions with us that must be regarded as having the potential to make a contribution to the good life and which is essential to a complete education. Unfortunately though, there can be pedagogical and logical problems when acquaintance knowledge has to be formalised into a curriculum specification. What follows is but one example.

MUSICAL KNOWLEDGE AND THE POLITICS OF THE CURRICULUM

Music in the curriculum is not only influenced by traditional practices, teachers and other educators. In many countries, accountability and 'commonsense' became political watchwords in the 1990s. Unfortunately, those in positions where they are able to determine educational policy have often not been able to think carefully through the kind of issues I am raising here and may indeed regard them as unnecessarily complex. Falling back on 'commonsense' – that is to say on unanalysed intuitive knowledge – avoids the onus of careful reflection and fails to take up and respond to the challenge of other ideas and ways of thinking. This can cause a deal of trouble, especially when music is to be fitted into a formal educational framework.

A striking example of this occurred in Britain between 1991 and 1992 when music was being admitted to the then new National Curriculum framework. Its significance goes well beyond the confines of the British educational system and shows how ill-conceived attitudes to musical knowledge can skew a curriculum. Britain is not the only country where a curriculum for music has been formalised and the careful reader from elsewhere can be forewarned and forearmed if necessary. The same kind of problems can occur at the level of a single school. This particular story goes thus.

A working group was set up to draft the National Curriculum music curriculum, the first time in Britain that music or indeed any school subject was to have a legally binding framework. The terms of reference for all subject working groups spell out the need to formulate clear attainment targets which are defined as:

... the knowledge, skills, understanding and aptitudes which pupils of different abilities and maturity should be expected to have acquired at or near certain ages.

(Department of Education and Science 1987a: Annex A)

The original emphasis in the general National Curriculum proposals was thus quite rightly upon articulating learning outcomes as central elements of course construction and pupil assessment. Further weight is given to these outcomes in the concept of 'profile components'. Attainment targets or profile components – the terms became increasingly confused over time – are seen as crucial elements 'that reflect the variety of knowledge, skills and understanding to which the subject gives rise' (DES 1987b: Section 35).

Here then was an opportunity for each subject group to declare the fundamental strands of its discipline. Aware of the importance of establishing some kind of knowledge basis, the working group for music initially attempted to expound a map of musical knowing not unrelated to the one I have already sketched out above (DES 1991a: 18). Unfortunately, this attempt was not consistently followed through and, in any case, during the whole process it became subject to the 'commonsense' beliefs of politicians and administrators lacking in experience of either music or education. Teachers and others were told that ministers had 'views' while educators had only 'theories'.

The music group's formal map of musical knowledge in the *Interim Report* was compromised by giving a list of attainment targets, where 'knowing' is specified as though it were a curriculum *activity* (DES 1991a).

PROFILE COMPONENT 1: MAKING MUSIC
Attainment Target 1 – Performing
Attainment Target 2 – Composing

PROFILE COMPONENT 2: UNDERSTANDING MUSIC
Attainment Target 3 – Listening
Attainment Target 4 – Knowing

The effect of this was to imply that 'knowing' was not part of performing and composing, that there is no 'understanding' in music-making. This model of musical knowledge – and it is a model – falls into the conceptual trap that had previously enticed most other subject groups: the failure to recognise that activities and learning outcomes are two quite different dimensions – process and product – both essential but in logically distinct categories. To specify an activity without stipulating the knowledge and understanding that might be acquired through and demonstrated in that activity is to devalue the activity and fail to articulate any educational purpose for it.

An activity without likely learning outcomes – a process without a sense of product – is a mindless, haphazard undertaking. Specifying 'knowing' as a separate process entity disconnects it from musical practice, encouraging a view of musical knowledge as merely propositional, factual – knowing *about* music rather than knowledge of music.

The activities that the music working group really appeared to be proposing were composing music, performing music, listening as audience to music and talking (or writing) about music, and that the last of these might best be subsumed into the others as an outcome of these activities. If these are the major activity strands of the music curriculum there remains a vacuum on the knowledge dimension: sensitivity to and control of sound materials, expressive character, form and value. We have no idea from the proposed structure of this curriculum as to the learning outcomes, those changes in the thought and feeling of students that may be taken away from the activities.

By August 1991 a *Final Report* laid out the triad of elements which had for a decade or more defined the fundamental activities of music as a British school subject. These were now called Composing, Performing and Appraising. The term appraising is carefully defined and refers specifically to the *audience-listener* role and carries with it the suggestion of musical criticism that in turn suggests some kind of educational rigour. In the Report 'appraisal' is tied in with what there is called 'relevant knowledge' of historical and cultural background (DES August 1991b).

> *Attainment Target 1 – Performing*
> *Attainment Target 2 – Composing*
> *Attainment Target 3 – Appraising*

Of course there are logical difficulties about this category set. Appraising is essential and central when people are composing and performing and may often be best developed and certainly best revealed through these activities. In any case, in terms of curriculum design (a) composing and performing are essentially activities and (b) clusters of activities really cannot be attainment targets. What has been attained is surely what has been *learned*, the residue left with us, some change of insight or level of responsiveness, that which we take away with us when an activity has ceased – in our case, musical knowledge. However, in a large-scale consultative exercise, most teachers and other musicians supported this formulation.

In a response attached to this *Final Report*, the Secretary of State for

Education asked a key advisory body, the National Curriculum Council, 'to avoid an excessive degree of complexity and prescriptiveness', suggesting to this end that 'there is a case for two attainment targets instead of three'. This theoretical fixation on the apparent relative simplicity of smaller numbers is sadly misplaced. Simplicity is not at all the same as effectiveness. If it were so, it might seem perfectly reasonable to reduce the essential three colours of red, blue and green that make up a television image to two. Why not get rid of, say, red? Surely it would make television manufacture simpler? Unfortunately it would also compromise the level of visual reproduction. On the same logical level, why not make chairs with two legs instead of three or four? If we really wanted to be simple in terms of a small number we could more reasonably specify just *one* attainment target, *knowing and understanding music*, define this properly and then specify the major classroom activities through which these outcomes are brought about.

The National Curriculum Council nonetheless took very seriously the ministerial suggestion of reducing the music attainment targets to two. The Council also responded to pressure to increase the status of propositional knowledge within the subject, relating this specifically to the western cultural heritage. This publication ignited a flurry of heat which raged around two fundamental issues. One of these was a shift in the direction of a more detailed study of western classical music by specifying particular composers for study in a detailed list of exemplars. The other was the reformulation of the attainment target titles and descriptions. This is in effect the National Curriculum Council's 'theory of musical knowledge' (National Curriculum Council, January 1992).

Attainment Target 1 – Performing and composing
The development of the ability to perform and compose music

Attainment Target 2 – Knowledge and understanding
The development of knowledge and understanding of musical history and theory, including the ability to listen to and appraise music

This model of musical knowledge is misleading. Musical knowledge is again made a travesty by being completely split off from musical action and is confined to the facts of history and 'theory'. Composing and performing seem to have become mindless activities in which understanding is neither acquired nor demonstrated; this is obvious nonsense.

In a series of exchanges – well-publicised on radio, TV and in the newspapers – the Secretary of State for Education was left in no doubt that the major impediment to professional acceptance of the report was the implication in the attainment targets that knowledge and understanding were essentially tied up with knowing about music and do not enter into the

appraising

activities of performing and composing. This may not have been intended but it was inescapable in the way that the attainment targets were being defined. Furthermore, the balance had been tipped heavily towards factual knowledge *about* music rather than knowledge *of* music by the actual wording of the second attainment target. This would have the likely effect of increasing the amount of disconnected factual information within a subject already restricted to a small corner of time in the school curriculum.

Listening to music and appraising (analysing) it are the keys to understanding music history. These activities should not be slipped in at the end of the target statement after the word 'including'. The use of the word 'theory' is also misleading. In Britain it seems to mean knowing about music notation and the rudiments of harmony, an activity which is not at all the same as being able actually to read and write music notation when composing and performing.

It was also suggested by the present writer (in a crucial and fortuitously timed fax) that the attainment targets should be re-worded and that the practical elements of the curriculum might be strengthened by specifying a time weighting in their favour (Swanwick 1992). The *Draft Order* of 27 January, 1992, carried these proposed new descriptions and there was a suggested weighting to Attainment Target 1 of 2:1 in favour of composing and performing (Department of Education and Science 1992).

Attainment Target 1 – Performing and composing
The development of the ability to perform and compose music with understanding

Attainment Target 2 – Listening and appraising
The development of the ability to listen to and appraise music, including knowledge of musical history

In a press release, the British Secretary of State commented that the argument about the attainment target structure was mostly 'about packaging rather than substance', but conceded that 'the acquisition of knowledge and understanding should not be separated from the practical activities'. For this reason he said he had 'changed the title of the second of the music attainment targets, and amended the longer description of both targets' along the lines suggested. This statement about packaging gives some indication of the level of understanding underpinning this particular theory of musical knowledge and it is sad to note that the art and design curriculum was left with 'making' divorced from knowledge and understanding, as though nothing had been learned from the music education debate.

A comparison of these formulations reveals profound differences in the definition of what counts as valuable knowledge and how it is acquired, revealed and assessed. Music or art history have to be approached through the doors and windows of particular pieces and performances, specific paintings and sculptures. Otherwise it is the history *not* of music or art but of musicians and artists, their lives and times, the chronology of musical instruments or studio techniques or a directory of musical types – rondo, fugue, blues and artistic genre.

If the historical model is dominant, then music is indeed likely to be played or a picture displayed not for its own sake but to illustrate something else; perhaps a particular tradition, period or style, or the life and times of a group or individual. The National Curriculum Council formulation could be seen as an invitation to substitute in large measure propositional knowledge, knowledge *that* for knowledge *of* music; a fact which becomes clear if we look at the amended programmes of study. The 'Orders' which place music and art in the British curriculum on a legal footing could be taken to be indicative of cultural tokenism, depending on our interpretation of them.

The Orders aim to introduce pupils to our cultural heritage and to give them an appreciation by the age of 14 of music and art history.

(Schools Update, Summer 1992).

If this really means an appreciation of music and art *history* then things are indeed adrift. Alternatively, if it is merely careless writing and really points to an appreciation of *music* and *art* from other times and places, then the declaration moves beyond both the study of history and cultural tokenism. The line here may appear to be fine but it is a significant demarcation of attitudes to music and musical knowledge and it separates two quite different attitudes to music teaching and learning.

It seems curious that decisions with statutory force affecting children in schools should be finally in the hands of people with no musical credentials and little relevant experience of music education. This whole episode might have been avoided if greater notice had been taken of work in the field, mapping out the structure of musical knowledge, and musical activities. The essential problem was a failure adequately to consider the nature of musical knowledge and a doctrinaire resistance to heed the views of many professionals and others who, by virtue of their experience, both intuitively and analytically recognise that knowing 'about' music too easily gains the upper hand.

Unfortunately, attempts to frame any music curriculum for schools often seem to take for granted the underlying musical knowledge base and frequently drift towards unattached propositional knowledge. In the USA, and without reference to any explicit rationale, a draft set of 'voluntary standards' analysed musical knowing into four 'sections'; since then reduced to three:

1 creation and performance;
2 cultural and historical context;
3 perception and analysis;
4 the nature and value of the arts.

(MENC 1993)

From the associated proposed curriculum detail, it becomes apparent that the second of these knowledge clusters could be largely accessed from books, that the third is substantially identified with notational skills and that the fourth – while making some reference to critical listening and value attitudes to music – involves a lot of contextual talk about conductors, instrument makers, and so on. This seems strange, especially following a lyrical introduction on the arts as 'an outlet for human creativity and self-expression'.

Furthermore, what is thought in pieces tends to be taught in segments. Should these 'sections' become operational in relative isolation, an underlying risk is of populations of children whose view of musical knowledge is filtered through a propositional model. It is so easy to substitute facts for sensitive action and analysis. There may also be a generation of teachers desensitised to the particularity of the intuitive/analytical dialectic through which musical meaning is construed.

Fortunately, in Britain, the worst errors were to some extent neutralised by hard work, quick responses and concerted professional action, which included widely disseminated public statements by well-known composers, conductors, musicians and music educators. This storm in a curriculum teacup can be seen partly as a power and status issue revolving around conflicting theories about the nature of musical knowledge, what 'counts' as music and who determines school music courses. The attempt to ignore professional values would not have been taken so far had education been a 'growth' area. Even so, the resistance to pressure on the music curriculum surprised those in other subjects, where in general there has been no sustained attempt by educators to identify the essential deep structures of knowledge. It might be inferred that teachers working in high status curriculum areas have been so protected by their traditional status and level of resource that there has been little pressure to think through the fundamentals. Under such conditions there may be no urgency to ask what are the essential knowledge dimensions, the real profile components of the subjects.

The situation is very different in the arts: partly to fend off curriculum marginalisation and to find a compelling professional rationale, arts educators are always turning over and disputing the nature and value of their activity, trying to articulate a 'philosophy', attempting to define and defend their knowledge base; hence a readiness to respond to the challenge.

I hope that these two examples of theories of musical knowledge in action have shown that it is important for music educators to expose intuitive understanding to analytical scrutiny. Analysis is not the prior imposition of a rigid framework on a free-range idea but a chosen and declared way of selecting data for attention and reading coherence into them. The disadvantages of unexamined intuition are obvious – especially when it is venerated as 'commonsense'.

Intuition and analysis are thus always interactive. As we have seen, this applies as much to the activity of research as to curriculum development, and it is research into music and music education which becomes the focus of the next part of this book.

Part II

Researching musical experience

4   Research and the magic of music

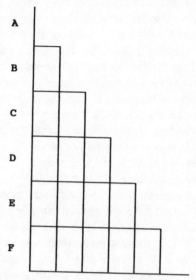

Figure 7   Birtwhistle's graph for his *Triumph of Time*
Note The Cor Anglais melody fulfils the role of 'A' in the diagram as it repeats three times unchanged in the piece.

MEASURING MOONBEAMS

The quotation, and graph in Figure 7, are from the 'unwritten notes' on the record sleeve by the composer Harrison Birtwhistle on his music, *The Triumph of Time* (1974). He tells us that the 'A' musical idea is an element that never changes while descending through a sequence of unlimited degrees of change. The title of the composition is borrowed from the etching by Peter Bruegel and this has beneath it the Latin motto, which translated means 'time devouring all and each'. In the etching, time, death and fame appear to be in a chaotic procession which leaves behind it the scattered remains of human endeavour.

> From left to right we can identify: the painter's palette and brush; the musician's instruments and compositions; the artisan's tools; the warrior's weapons; the crown of the king, the helmet of the knight, the hats of the cleric and the burgher; then sword, scepter, and pruning shears; the broken column of a church or temple; a treasure chest, a money bag.
>
> (Klein 1963: 176)

Perhaps this procession of time is the 'A' idea of Birtwhistle's piece? But why does he not leave us alone with his music? Why does he explain and describe and draw pictures of his compositional agenda in the form of a graph? Why not have a blank record sleeve? The urge to probe, interpret and explain is universal. Birtwhistle is engaging in secondary analysis, re-searching his own compositional process. His picture came after the music, as did his awareness of the existence of the Bruegel etching. Of course, his graph tells us less than the composition itself but it has the possibility of informing our response to the music. It is an analytical slice across the work which highlights just a part of the whole. Like any kind of analysis, this graph tells us less than everything about the object of attention but it brings to mind something that might otherwise escape our notice – a sense of continuous line in a piece of music that can sound fragmented.

Graphic illustrations do not prove anything but they are suggestive of relationships. I wish to get this clear right at the start of this part of the book, for later on there will be a number of graphic illustrations of research findings. These pictures of data should be regarded in the same way as the drawing by Harrison Birtwhistle. They illustrate in a simple form certain cross-sections of observed phenomena. We cannot pretend that displays of data can be substituted for musical experience itself, but they are representations of particular aspects of the phenomenon of musical engagement and they have the potential to deepen our understanding of the nature and acquisition of musical knowledge.

> We can all agree that direct experience in music education is far more important than any attempt to quantitatively *or* qualitatively describe the events taking place. But to confuse an event with a description of the event... is to ask too much of systematic investigation of any kind.
>
> (Heller and Campbell 1985: 30)

It may be tempting to shrug off the whole idea of trying scientifically to study or analyse what may appear to be the almost magical power of music. Are we trying to weigh a moonbeam or measure a thought? Can the clanking apparatus of the social sciences really throw light on intuitive knowledge? Experiments and associated statistical analysis are sometimes seen as just crude, 'an accurate reflection of the incompatibility of the concept of meas-urement when applied to human social settings' (Reimer 1985: 13). Reimer leans heavily in the direction of the intuitive, interpretative paradigm, pro-testing that every human being is unique and that nature cannot be understood 'by reducing its complexities to underlying mechanical principles' (p.1). But we know that intuitive ingenuity itself reduces the complexities of the buzzing confusion of sensory events into patterns, into images, into organising perspectives. (We have no need to drag the emotive word 'mechanical' into the argument.)

Even so, reliance only on intuitive knowledge has its own limits. Intuitively we certainly see things as a whole but always from one personal point of view, and we can be intuitively wrong. To claim infallibility for holistic interpretations of intuition would be to go too far. This is why we sometimes need less ambitious but detailed analytical work to test out our hunches. The small experiment with the first paragraph of *In the South* allowed us to claim only that many children were able to describe certain expressive and structural characteristics with more certainty, merely by further acquaintance with the music accompanied by a request for an 'analysis' on a simple form. Intuitively we might have already come to this unpretentious and limited insight; but unless we are prepared to observe a little more carefully what children themselves tell us about their musical experience we ought to be circumspect about jumping to conclusions.

We need observation, detailed evidence, analysis to test out intuitive hunches. The paraphernalia of scientific research should not be dismissed out of hand simply because it will never tell us everything all at once. The magic of music is not spoiled by curiosity and careful enquiry into how it works in our minds and the minds of others, provided that we know when to draw back. An analysis of musical experience is not a substitute for that experience and the reverse is also true: intuitive musical experience can tell us nothing about itself without analysis.

We are all at some time or other researchers in attitude, asking questions that begin with 'why?', 'how?', 'what would happen if?'. And we all have theories that we bring to the general data of living, available evidence and indeed to specific activities like composing. Without such conjectures any activity – including making music or teaching – would become mechanical, mindless. Composers have views about the compositional process and many have expressed these very eloquently as theories in letters, books and programme notes. Consciously or unconsciously we are always looking for patterns of meaning, we weave theories and sift through data. There is no such thing as theoretical neutrality and there is certainly no such thing as unbiased research. Evidence is inevitably seen and to some extent constructed through the apparatus of mind that belongs uniquely to the participant. But research does not take these perspectives or theories for granted, as if they were carved in stone or sanctified by some mysterious entity called 'commonsense'. After all, it once was 'commonsense' that the earth was flat, an idea that works quite well if we want to plough a field but is of more limited use if we are to send a rocket to the moon and get it back again. In taking on a research attitude we are required to probe a little, to test out theories and challenge 'commonsense' assumptions.

Can any activity be research? Artists and composers may claim that in producing works of art or composing they are themselves researching – exploring new territory, shaping ideas in a public form. It is possible to make the same claim for teaching; that it is a constant reshaping of materials, activities and teaching styles to meet changing circumstances, and that in the act of developing curriculum activities a teacher is by definition a researcher.

The case for regarding artistic activity as a form of research has been made by Elliot Eisner who distinguishes between scientific and artistic research modes (Eisner 1981). Arguing correctly that all empirical research is essentially qualitative – in that it aims to describe, interpret or predict qualities – he traces the arts/science distinction on several levels. The scientific paradigm he sees as being characterised by the quest for emotional neutrality, by a tendency to quantify findings, to be able to predict or control, to set up standardised procedures such as tests, to seek for laws or general principles and to report any findings in formal ways through discursive or 'knowing that' descriptions and propositions.

On the other hand, for Eisner, validity of research in the arts mode is 'the persuasiveness of a personal vision', not reducing information to generalisations or average tendencies but seeing things whole. Artistic research is 'less concerned with the discovery of truth than with the creation of meaning'. This meaning is made public embodied in vivid images, in sustained metaphors.

QUALITY OR QUANTITY?

In his more recent writing, Elliot Eisner moves towards identifying the artistic approach to research even more closely with the qualitative concept (Eisner 1991). For him the overall character of a qualitative study is that it is field focused rather than laboratory based, and that the researcher is seen as an instrument with an interpretative role and not as a neutral gatherer of data. Reporting this kind of research invites the use of expressive language, giving attention to particulars and seeking coherence, insight and instrumental utility (pp. 32–40).

This philosophical conflict – as here expressed by Eisner – sporadically rages around research in the social sciences. The polarities – sometimes referred to as normative and interpretative and as quantitative or qualitative – each place a different weight on the possibility of the objectivity of the researcher and on more subjective interpretations of situations. Cohen and Manion draw our attention to the dimensions of this apparent dichotomy and we can immediately see that we are into the same old unhelpful polarity between the claims of intuitive and analytical knowledge (Cohen and Manion 1980: 25). Knowledge arising through the activity we call research has its own left–right tensions. My purpose is to suggest that both sides of the analytical/intuitive spectrum are engaged interactively in research.

Differing approaches to research

Interpretative	*Normative*
The individual	Society and the social system
Human actions continuously re-creating social life	Impersonal forces regulating behaviour
'Subjectivity'	'Objectivity'
Interpreting the specific	Generalising from the specific
Understanding actions	Explaining behaviour
Investigating the taken-for-granted	Assuming the taken-for-granted
(Based on Cohen and Manion 1980)	

Essentially, what is called the normative perspective is a search for general theories or explanations into which data may fit. This sometimes strikes people as being 'hard-nosed'. Indeed, there is a danger that both techniques and findings may be insensitively forced into a rigid pre-existing framework or even that we may ignore quite obvious features of a situation because of our previously acquired explanatory blinkers. Sensitive ways of gathering data and respect for subjects as people might be safeguards to some extent and even cause us to revise any initial theory. We have to be careful of taking things for granted, especially our conceptual framework.

The interpretative – the so-called qualitative approach – would have us stay close to the observer's holistic, intuitive perception and resist generalisations, preferring to stay with the richness of unique and particular cases rather than spreading out into broad surveys or laboratory-type experiments. The problem with this is the difficulty of saying what we have learned *beyond* the detail of any specific instance. Studying the musical activities of only one or two children may give us insights into their musical behaviour and observing just one classroom may stimulate us to think about group interactions. But such findings require a very delicate interpretation and we need larger samples before we can more confidently say anything more *in general*, either about the ways in which children learn or about social dynamics. This can limit the usefulness of findings. In any case, the interpretative researcher must eventually work to some explanatory code which allows certain explanations rather than others. We can never avoid a selective perspective; there is no such thing as an innocent eye or neutral data.

The resemblance of the interpretative/normative polarities to Croce's analysis of knowledge into intuitive and analytical categories is surely no coincidence. There seems to be a tension between the desire on one hand to explain, categorise and generalise; and on the other hand to intuitively and holistically savour specific *things* – to be immersed in the delight of the here-and-now, engrossed in the integrity of the particular. There is a poem by Walt Whitman, *When I Heard the Learn'd Astronomer*, in which he describes how he went to a lecture where the audience was shown charts and diagrams representing the solar system, 'to add, divide, and measure them'. He concludes the poem thus.

How soon unaccountable I became tired and sick,
Till rising and gliding out I wandered off by myself,
In the mystical moist night air, and from time to time,
Looked up in perfect silence at the stars.

It is easy to sympathise with this romantic attitude. But making sense of the world requires that we are both poet and astronomer, artist and scientist, bringing the intuitive and the logical into a dynamic relationship. An intuitive sense of what is appropriate helps us to steer towards worthwhile questions and to find a sound approach for tackling them; it helps us avoid missing 'the wood for the trees'. Conversely, detailed analytical method can clarify and feed back into the intuitive realm. The universe is no less puzzling and exciting to us who live in a post moon-landing era than it was to Ancient Greek astronomers. Music is no less magical because we have ideas and some evidence as to how and why it affects us. Whatever Birtwhistle's graph tells us about his piece, it certainly does not invalidate the composition and may even be helpful.

There is though a fundamental difference between the scientific and artistic paradigm – not mentioned by Eisner – and which concerns our attitudes to the relationship between theory and data. A painter or composer is at liberty to alter an evolving picture or score, to change the 'data', to fit an intuitive hunch of how it might become. That would be true to the spirit of artistic making. On the contrary, a scientific attitude does not permit us to change data to fit our theories. That would be dishonest. Here the artist differs from those engaged in research. For example, it would not do for a researcher to propose some view of how children respond to music, without ever observing or asking them, or making some attempt to find patterns in the detail of these observations.

While I have no serious objection to calling composing, writing, painting or even curriculum development 'research', it might be better not to totally identify the making of art works (or drafting educational plans) with systematic, structured enquiry. Eisner again:

... when you want to know how many students dropped out of a high school class you don't want a set of sonnets, you want a set of numbers.... The field of education in particular needs to avoid methodological monism.

(Eisner 1981: 9)

Put another way: the apparently opposite claims of rationality and intuition in research 'constitute an epistemological continuum, not a dichotomy' (Miles and Huberman 1984). Research neither destroys the magic of music nor trivialises educational transactions. On the contrary it can be a way of caring for and understanding something of both. There is no such thing as free-standing data, uninterpreted by people; people having minds tinged with affect and shaped by personal histories, people hoping for certain outcomes, people looking for and creating meaning for themselves – meaning with its source in intuitive understanding and analytically articulated. Research is one way of subjecting intuitive insights to analytical scrutiny.

RESEARCH PROCESSES

A whole repertoire of techniques has evolved to meet the aspiration of research to be a way of bringing what is hidden into the open, to articulate and develop intuitive hunches. There are general criteria for engaging in research and many specific methods open to researchers. I need to briefly review these, drawing attention to the relationship between the interpretative and normative paradigms in any method.

There are fairly obvious conditions under which research can be set up and evaluated. The first criterion is that research should contribute to developing a base of professional knowledge. There seems little point in doing systematic work on the effectiveness of clarinet teaching methods, or designing tests of musical ability, or digging away at the history of *sol-fa*, unless we place and interpret these in a professional perspective. Otherwise we shall end up with rather dreary lists of theses and projects, a state of fragmentation with each researcher isolated from the other inside a tiny issue of little real interest or relevance, lacking quality.

The second criterion is that we make explicit that data are being viewed in a particular way. The conceptual framework must be declared, assumptions have to be brought out on to the table. For example, if we happened to be devising tests of musical aptitude, have we given thought to what we really mean by either 'musical' or 'aptitude'; do we just assume they involve pitch and rhythmic discrimination or what? It is essential to limit any enquiry to the scale of what is manageable but in the interests both of professional development and relevance a larger canvas should always be discernible, the work should lie within range of intuitive vision. This is why the small experiment described earlier was located within the wider problem of the nature of musical knowledge. The limited hypothesis and the practical experimental problems stemmed from a more fundamental question.

Thirdly, a research method has to be articulated that promotes a certain level of analytical objectivity beyond that with which we normally operate from day to day. The very idea of structured enquiry centres on this aspiration towards objectivity. We can never manoeuvre ourselves into a state of total neutrality but we can see that precautions are taken to establish careful control in any research method and a degree of critical 'objectivity' in our interpretations of the findings. A good researcher is self-critical, keeping in mind both the relevance or *validity* of the assumptions and the likelihood of replicating the findings, the *reliability* of the method.

Fourthly, the results of any investigation have to be shared with others. This does not necessarily imply publication in a learned journal but there ought to be some way in which results become openly available. Public sharing makes it possible to test and criticise the work, perhaps even to replicate it, in order to re-examine the credibility of the method and the interpretation of the findings. In any case, the results may be of professional significance. If nothing follows, then why bother?

A fifth criterion is quite simply that research should be conducted in a spirit of 'phil-osophy' – a love of knowledge. This ideal is not always easy to attain, especially when research is contracted out by funding bodies rather than chosen. But 'phil-osophy' is an important touchstone which may head us off from temptations to conceal or falsify evidence or misinterpret findings. It safeguards 'quality'.

It becomes fairly clear what research is *not*. It is certainly not stating personal convictions without reasoning them through or presenting relevant evidence; it is not quoting the views of others without critical comment or synthesis; it is not the narration of selected anecdotes or quotations from 'authorities' to support a case; it is not merely amassing statistics. Nor is it the expression of the already obvious in difficult language, as when the beginning of the Biblical 23rd Psalm is translated into such jargon as:

> The Lord and I are in a shepherd/sheep situation, and I am in a position of negative need; he conducts me directionally parallel to non-torrential aqueous liquid.

It may have been Francis Bacon who said that we are more likely to reach the truth through error than confusion. We should try to express error in a clear and lively fashion, the more easily recognised for what it is when stripped of unnecessary jargon and equivocating obfuscation. A research attitude includes a impulse towards clarity both of process and expression, and is characterised by openness to intuitive insight and a willingness to engage in critical analysis. Near the start of any research – ideally – we should be able to say:

> I have identified an area that seems important, interests me and is professionally relevant, and I have specified a starting point that at least gets me going. I am prepared to live for a time with uncertainty about details of methodology but I am able to articulate a question which will focus my work. I formulate this as a question because it is healthier to attempt to answer a question than to elaborate an answer I already think I know.

A number of well-tried procedures are open to researchers. We shall meet up with some of these later as they inform our understanding of music and music education. I have here to acknowledge their existence in a very brief overview – not comprehensive but indicative. During this review it should become apparent that the interpretative *versus* normative issue is really a bogus problem.

Research can take on any or all of the following forms, none of which can stand without regard both for the integrity of 'subjective' interpretation and the 'objectivity' of declared analytical frames.

1 *Conceptual analysis and synthesis is the process of reflecting, classifying, inspecting the logical structure of arguments, testing a theory for internal validity. The essential process here is deduction, discussion about a set of relationships, forming a conceptual framework.*

Strictly speaking, establishing a conceptual framework is not a discrete method. It is part of *all* good research. Indeed, it makes research 'good'. It is possible to conduct an enquiry that goes no further than reasoned and structured argument based on the process of deduction and logical inference, along the lines of philosophy or mathematics. This procedure is more frequently encountered in certain central European traditions than in the research cultures of Anglo-American empiricism or pragmatism.

Yet we often run into problems of conceptual clarification in music education. They are embodied in such questions as; 'what is musicianship?' or, 'is music education aesthetic education?'. A good example of this kind of research procedure would be an analysis of the concept of 'listening'. For example, Brian Loane argues a particular viewpoint which leads him to the conclusion that 'audience-listening is beyond the reach of assessment, and therefore of teaching interaction' (Loane 1984). But a little empirical work – 'on the ground' – into audience-listening may cause us to question such a statement. All philosophers give examples (data?). There is no such thing as a pure 'thought experiment', detached from lived experience and observation. The ways in which people listen to music may be complex but they are not entirely beyond reach of assessment. However, Loane has helpfully cleared the theoretical ground a little.

Conceptual 'ground clearing' is essential in any piece of work – no matter how practical or empirical the method. Confusion abounds when concepts remain unexamined – for example, where the same words may be taken at face value as meaning the same thing although the contexts may be very different.

A good example would be the equation of 'literacy' in the linguistic sense with 'musical (notational) literacy'. These are quite different concepts and we would need to probe these differences. For instance, it may indeed be essential that all children learn to read and write but is it essential that they all learn to read and write *music*? And what does this mean? When we read a page of a book is this the same kind of process as 'reading' the accompaniment of a song? What is the relationship between literacy and being articulate – for example, are there differences in being literate as a singer, or on the bassoon, or the bass guitar? Can we be musically educated even if we do not read staff notation?

2 *Observation and log-keeping is the systematic recording of events, as when studying the natural habits of creatures or in ethnographic or anthropological study of human communities.*

Of all research processes, observation is perhaps the closest to daily life. We all 'people watch'. The ethnographic observer to some degree lives 'with the tribe' (ethnos = people or race; graphy = description). Observing the work of children or inter-personal relationships in schools would fall into this category. While it is certainly possible to write fairly intuitively about what we see, we need to acknowledge that there is such a thing as a neutral, naive observer. Our selection of what we *choose* to observe – and therefore what we exclude from our observations – depends on our particular theoretical perspective, as does the way we interpret these observations. The interpretation of behavioural 'quantity' depends on a prior qualitative assessment.

To make sense of any complex activity – say work in a classroom – requires an element of filtering and categorisation. If the structure of an interpretation is left to emerge *after* the event, then the research process may be described as 'qualitative' and the conceptual stance as 'grounded theory' (Strauss 1987). We observe in as unprejudiced a way as possible and try to make sense of what we see. This 'making sense' will inevitably involve the reduction of data into manageable form by the process of analysis and, inevitably, quantification; at least to the extent that certain strands of data come to be seen to be relatively more significant than others. The essential rule is to refrain from hypothesising, creating theories in advance – a state of mind which is ideal rather than achievable.

Alternatively we can devise schemes of systematic observation – looking at teaching and learning through pre-arranged analytical filters. The simplest kind of system is to record specific types of event – for example, how many times children actually make music in music lessons, or how frequently a choral or band director draws attention to expressive as distinct from technical features of music. Structured observation reduces interpretation to manageable proportions but at the risk of missing important events that may not be part of any categorisation system. Filters are bound to exclude some potential data, depending on the size and shape of the mesh.

Detailed study of particular *cases* is a favoured method in education and can be part of any observational strategy. We can study as cases an individual, a group of people, an institution or a particular event – such as a music festival. A well-written case study can give us the 'shock of reality' but will suffer from local limitations. It is very difficult to generalise outwards from a single case study, or even from multiple cases. All depends on the conceptual framework in the mind of the observer and the integrity of the analysis (Yin 1989). Two good examples of very influential case students would be Freud and Piaget, both of whom worked with a small number of people (cases) – patients and children respectively – but used these observations to develop and exemplify theories of mind and knowledge respectively.

We can observe without intended intervention, trying to emulate a fly on the wall as nearly as possible. We can also see ourselves as part of the action, as indeed were Freud and Piaget. The action might include asking stimulating or probing questions, or introducing new ideas or material as a teacher, perhaps attempting to evaluate its effect on the attitudes and understanding of the students. Action research takes us away from the cool detachment of distance, involving us more directly with the people we study. Potential information may be rich but can easily become unmanageable and may be strongly biased – unless we are very careful in our interventions and interpretation.

Although action research is sometimes seen as the antithesis of controlled experimental work, observing the effects of *any* intervention is really a humanised variation of an experimental research process – though in a rich and complex setting. Many researchers are interested in seeing 'what happens when', 'what happens if'. Action research differs from other forms of experimentation in that the researcher is an 'actor' in the arena of enquiry – a level of involvement that does not automatically guarantee 'authenticity'. 'Quality' in research depends not only on intuitively governed actions but also on the analytical ability of the researcher.

3 *Experiment is the classic 'scientific' model: observing the effect of a controlled intervention, usually linked with a prediction – that a change*

in certain conditions will result in a change in something else – though we could be uncertain which way things might go. The paradigm is essentially horticultural and involves making comparisons. We plant seeds, fertilise some, leave others alone, and measure differences in growth, controlling the laboratory conditions of heat, humidity, soil and light, manipulating only the 'independent' variable (the type of fertiliser) and measuring the 'dependent' variable (the size of the crop).

Measurement of organic growth – whilst fairly easy with a rule calibrated in centimetres or inches – is not easily transferred to the social sciences, where there is often no conventionally agreed index of measurement. With what rule do we measure liking for music, technical efficiency, aesthetic understanding or grasp of style? How do we calibrate attitudes to the choir, band or general class music? One answer is to devise tests and music educators have indeed devised them, especially tests of musical ability where it was sometimes forgotten that aural discriminations of pitch or rhythm are but a small corner of the universe of musical experience. As I tried to show in the first chapter, musical knowledge is much more than making aural discriminations. Furthermore, we ought not to confuse experimenting with testing even though the application of standard tests is a beguiling way of measuring the changes caused by intervention.

The worth of such measures depends utterly on the validity of the measuring instrument, which – in the social sciences – is not as easy to come by or as dependable as a rule or a thermometer. For instance, we really cannot deduce from test results that rhythmic ability in children develops before melodic memory and that both appear before harmonic awareness (Bentley 1966). We have no idea of how to compare the results of any measure we might use for rhythm discrimination against any score we happen to get for pitch. These are two quite different tests and all we can say is that subjects score higher or lower on one test rather than another. But the tests may not be of equal difficulty, they may be scored on totally different scales of measurement. We have no way of knowing, unless we can come up with a convincing theory of musical mind which can connect the disparate elements into a framework of logical relationships.

The evaluation of music curriculum activities 'on the ground' seems experimentally much more promising than testing people in an isolated 'laboratory' context. There is something potentially attractive about the prospect of assessing the effect of a curriculum intervention, perhaps by comparison with a control group who are not taking part in the experimental programme. Imagine, for instance, that we wanted to find out whether children's knowledge of Birtwhistle's *Triumph of Time* is enhanced if audience-listening were preceded by compositional and performance work focusing on timbre, texture, levels of intensity, or on what Birtwhistle calls 'the overall image of the procession'. Can we be sure that the two groups are really matched for comparison? We also have to look very carefully at what the control group is doing. It would be experimentally and ethically unsound to treat the experimental group to the most intense musical experiences we could possible arrange and – over the same period of time – bore the others with an aimless activity.

Any experiment requires us to establish a level of external validity. There are crucial questions. Can the effect be generalised beyond the particular setting in which it took place – from one group of people to another? Is the experiment so artificial that nothing remotely like it exists in the world beyond? Is the effect under observation substantively related to the underlying assumptions? Are the indices of observation dependably linked to the focal issue? Does an attitude inventory meaningfully measure disposition to other people, to literature, music, political issues or to curriculum intervention – perhaps to new materials or a way of organising a classroom? External validity can never be fully assured and depends on our confidence in what Campbell and Stanley call the 'relevant laws' (Campbell and Stanley 1963: 17). Does replication of an experiment strengthen this confidence? Is there supporting evidence from elsewhere? Do we have a coherent theoretical rationale which makes generalisability at least likely?

There are other variables to be taken into account. We have to ask what else might be happening alongside the intervention: are pupils maturing or perhaps changing their attitudes because of growing familiarity with the school, their teachers and the curriculum generally? Does the experimental group feel 'special'? Is the experimenter putting any 'spin' on the research? Why has this group been selected in the first place? In spite of these problems there may be benefits from carrying out this kind of work, not least in terms of curriculum development in that it forces us all to think more carefully about classroom settings and the musical encounters that may or may not be taking place there.

A more naturalistic process than comparing groups is to study the effect of an intervention on the *same* group or individual over time, a time–series experiment (Campbell and Stanley 1963). Teachers inevitably work in this way as they observe (as participants) over days, weeks, months; estimating what difference a new activity, or a way of relating to students, or a set of materials seems to make. Repeated observations here act as a built-in control and this design seems ideally suited to the teacher-researcher, though it does require some patience, for we need to start careful observations some time before intervening. One-off interventions evaluated by single observations tell us nothing about whether or not any significant change is taking place.

As I shall show later, research in music education can profitably draw upon the method of repeated observations over time and on forms of analysis and data display that permit us to find or rule out particular patterns and relationships (Kratochwill 1978).

4　*Product analysis consists in looking at things that are made or said, such as the artifacts of Ancient Greeks or Romans, examining the painting, writing or music-making of children, analysing tapes of children's language or their written solutions to mathematical problems; documentary and historical research.*

Product evaluation is non-interactive, it takes place at a distance. We cannot, for example, influence the behaviour of the dead, only modify our own interpretation of their actions. Historical scholarship is the obvious example of searching products for meaning, where deductive processes are brought to bear on aural or documentary evidence. For some this may be one of the most beguiling forms of enquiry, since reading about other people in other places and at other times is in itself intrinsically fascinating. It will however not rise above the level of participation in well-documented gossip unless we are able to bring some form of analysis to bear that relates scraps of evidence into patterns.

For example, a researcher might look at the development of bands and orchestras in schools – assembling documentary evidence as to the growth or diminution of these activities over certain periods of time. The organisation and success of such groups might be seen to relate strongly to the work of particular individuals or to levels of funding or to general patterns of school management. To what extent have such groups developed because of the availability of less expensive instruments or of culturally acceptable repertoires, or because of persuasion by instrument-makers and music publishers? Is there a relationship between performing groups in schools and musical communities outside schools and does this appear to have changed over time? What happens to people's musical life when they leave?

Later, I shall be looking carefully at the musical products of children – their compositions and performances – and at the way they construe music as listeners. As is the case in historical work, there is much to be said for asking people who are not participants in the action to reflect upon and interpret the evidence – sensitive, independent observers can help us make sense of children's compositions or performances. However, Eisner questions this use of judges and – while conceding that consensus 'breeds confidence in the objectivity of the judgements rendered' – concludes that 'consensus provides no purchase on reality' (1991: 45).

Agreement can be facilitated in several ways. One is to simplify the object or qualities judged so that they require no interpretation or subtlety of perception; this is called low-inference data. The other is to create a set of restrictions that limit the scope for judgement so that its use is unnecessary and even impossible.

(Eisner 1991: 47)

Among these 'restrictions', Eisner might presumably include pre-specified criteria for assessing musical performances and compositions. Since I shall be describing research making extensive use both of independent observers and of criterion statements it seems important to answer this point. What Eisner calls 'educational criticism' surely depends by definition on developing and sharing *criteria*. Educational criticism can be at different levels, from an individual trying to describe and interpret the whole web of discourse in a classroom to an appraisal of the specific things students say, do or make. If specific criteria are automatically regarded as constricting or seen as setting up 'stock responses', we run the risk of never being able to make an educational decision. The belief that we have to wait for the 'whole picture' to emerge is not only impractical but asks for an impossibility. We never see the whole picture. We only see *our* picture. A willing acceptance of this limitation is crucial for all researchers and is central in the tradition of hermeneutics, which seeks coherence in the evidence of 'text' through the art of interpretation (Dilthey and Gadamer in Connerton 1976).

Setting forth well-founded assessment criteria is one way of engaging with and interpreting the work of students and is an invitation to professional sharing. It depends on the richness and rightness of the criteria, on their validity and on the reliability of the observers – whether or not there is any measure of agreement between what Eisner calls 'competent others' (Eisner 1991: 112).

5 *Verbal enquiry includes asking questions, surveying, interviewing, devising a questionnaire or attitude inventory. It may be part of any form of research but can be free-standing.*

A good deal of research in education is of the survey kind, intended to tease out such things as the level of provision, conditions under which people work and attitudes towards subjects, schools and so on. With what high expectations do we send out questionnaires and with what irritation do we receive those others send us! Here we are one step removed from the scene of action in that we do not directly observe the behaviour of students or teachers but ask them to describe to us their behaviour and attitudes. Imagine a written description by teachers of what takes place in their school music programme and compare this account with what *actually* happens. Then imagine that the written description is structured by a series of ticks and crosses in a carefully designed questionnaire. We are obviously likely to lose a great deal of information and pick up a few distorted signals on the way.

A fairly common procedure in educational research is to take 'free' responses of children – perhaps asking them to write what they think about music or school. We can then separate these out into single statements and get colleagues – independent observers – to remove those that seem ambiguous, sorting the remaining cards into piles of similar views. From this 'sort' it may be possible to identify representative categories to help in both the construction and analysis of an attitude inventory. Samples of these statements can be given to children of a similar age and in a similar setting, thus collecting a more tightly structured response from a larger population.

We may believe that we could guess the results without going to all this trouble; after all, every teacher has a perception of the general attitude or level of work of a class. It is important though to give the opportunity of expression to the silent or relatively silent majority. It is tempting for us to be influenced by those students who express their views easily, quickly, and perhaps loudly. Surveys and attitude inventories are democratically important instruments and a careful interpretation of results may often surprise us.

Interviews are more sensitive forms of verbal enquiry, a technique that is able to take us deeper into the thinking of other people – though at the risk of collecting data that spreads and may become awkward to interpret. Such structured conversations can be helpful in trying to understand how people construe music, and I shall return to interviews later, giving instances of some outcomes of this particular research process.

Research problems are always rooted in intuitive understanding before they pass through the mills of analysis and return as harvest to the intuitive granary – sometimes even becoming part of 'commonsense'. This cyclic process produces and revitalises the 'space between' the apparent polarities of interpretative and normative paradigms; the place where ideas are fashioned, disputed, traded and formulated into systems of belief, of thought; the realm of symbolic discourse.

Those who have been through the fire of systematic enquiry may not always produce striking findings, but that they are changed by the experience is certain and they look at their world differently. In one sense, the researcher is always the first of his or her own findings. A 'quality' experience is the reward when an intuitive sense of how things may be is informed by scientific curiosity and detailed technical analysis. What marks research out from 'commonsense' is the willingness to respond to critical scrutiny, to analyse intuitive insight, to have second thoughts. And the method must be plural. Here I agree with Reimer.

In addition to studies using the traditional research modes many should be attempted that break the old configurations by combining several modes within a single study and by inventing alternatives and by reaching out to related disciplines for both methodological and conceptual innovations.

(Reimer 1985: 17)

But who is actually doing this and is their work likely to be highly regarded by the 'establishments' of entrenched methodological positions? 'Inventing alternatives' happens to be my personal agenda – an aim that guides the shape, style and content of this book. Was it necessary to have spent so much time in the earlier chapters on conceptual, philosophical mapping? My answer has to be, yes, of course. The emergent view of musical knowledge underpins any empirical research I have to report. Was it necessary to have sketched out 'a fool's guide' to research methods? Again, I must say, yes. These instruments of investigation are crucial to any work out there in the field. I am unwilling to assume that everyone automatically shares the broad definition of research methodology which guides the practicalities of the enterprises I am discussing.

I can now rejoin my own research trail – a path that has already been opened up but which can now be followed into new territory. A crucial question has been: what is musical knowledge? The process of getting into such a question is essentially conceptual and this has been the main procedure in the first part of this book. A second concern is how musical knowledge comes to be acquired – the main focus of these present chapters and a question requiring consideration of more empirical evidence. This leads to a third issue: how music education might best be organised and conducted to assist in the process of the growth of knowledge.

Methods for working on these problems are bound to be diverse, taking account of the energy that is generated between the positive and negative poles of the intuitive and analytical. If not, then things start to go wrong. As Bronowski said long ago:

It has been one of the most destructive modern prejudices that art and science are different and somehow incompatible interests. We have fallen into the habit of opposing the artistic to the scientific temper; we even identify them with a creative and critical approach.

(Bronowski 1951)

In the necessary exchange between the research paradigms labelled 'qualitative' and 'quantitative'; in the cross-fertilisation of what Eisner calls artistic and scientific research modes, lies the possibility of finding Pirsig's 'quality' – where subject and object meet. For no productive scientist lacks intuitive vision and no effective artist gets by without analytical power. The researcher needs to be both scientist and artist. Whatever the method, intuitive scanning and analytical sifting go hand in hand.

5 The development of musical knowledge

CHARTING THE GROWTH OF KNOWLEDGE

In 1986 we reported research into the musical development of children as evidenced in their composing (Swanwick and Tillman 1986, Swanwick 1988). In this chapter I shall relate on-going work with that developmental spiral, showing its relationship to the intuitive/analytical dialectic already seen in action in musical experience and across research paradigms. Since 1986 there has been some interest in this account of the growth of children's musical knowledge and many valued comments and questions have been raised in response to that study. There have also been some misunderstandings which need attention here. In any event, there is now further work to report which seems to confirm and extend the original findings.

The theoretical basis arose in typical intuitive fashion. After years of worrying at the psychological basis of the arts, while on holiday thinking of nothing in particular, it became clear to me that artistic knowledge is not a domain of knowledge segregated from the rest of the activities of mind but draws its substance from the same deep psychological wells as science, philosophy and all other forms of symbolic discourse. After a further period of analysis I argued that essential psychological elements in all artistic engagement are the deep and universal processes of a desire for mastery, and an urge towards imitation, imaginative play and meta-cognition (Swanwick 1983). Although there are complications about this particular terminology – some of which I shall address later on – it was thought that these psycho-logi-cal processes have corresponding artistic elements; in music these are: perceiving and controlling sound materials, projecting and locating expressive character, awareness of dynamic structure and valuing. This combination of psychological and musical analysis needs some further clarification, we have already seen the musical strands at work in the performance, practice and criticism of music; in jazz, rock, western classical traditions and in observations on Maori and Venda music.

Although the emergent map of musical development came to be premised on these elements of musical experience, the actual detail of the developmental sequence was not at first apparent to us. It was not predicted but discovered. The compositions of children were not shoe-horned into pre-existing slots; rather the eventual detailed configuration grew out of attempts to understand the children's music in a qualitative way. Once again, empirical data – the evidence of observations – causes a review of a theoretical hunch.

If the conceptual background lay in a particular view of the nature of musical knowledge, the research foreground consisted of compositions produced by children, mostly, though not exclusively, aged 3 to 11 years. They came from many different ethnic and cultural groups, including Asian, West Indian, African, northern and southern European backgrounds, and they took part in regular class music lessons during which all had opportunities to make music in a variety of ways and at different levels of complexity. When they said their work was ready the pieces were recorded on tape, an activity which continued over four years, nine times each year, yielding 745 compositions from 48 children. We thus had a cross-section of music made by children of different ages and in some cases a longitudinal spectrum of compositions from individual children over a fairly long period of time.

The data – these compositions – were the subject of much intuitive scanning before any analytical pattern emerged. Four years of work with children is not a laboratory experiment. While respecting the unique quality of each composition we were keen to go beyond single case studies which, while offering special insights into particular compositions, do not easily lend themselves to creating any kind of map to help us observe and respond to individuals, develop a curriculum, plan music teaching or develop valid student assessment procedures.

When mapping the developmental spiral it was certainly not our aim to explain away the magic of musical experience or to underplay the uniqueness of individuals. A large area of musical knowledge is grasped holistically, subjective, submerged. It reaches the parts that many other educational activities cannot reach and obviously has deep roots in the aesthetic, with all the intuitive scanning and tacit, unarticulated meanings that flow from the dynamic relationship of individuals with significant objects or events. Each musical encounter is in a sense unique, never to be repeated, a rich transaction taking place simultaneously at the levels of the sensuous, the expressive and structurally coherent. This is why the consummation of musical experience is recognised in some cultures as being transcendental; it takes us out of ourselves and at the same time makes more of us.

But when we are thinking about music and music education we inevitably draw on logical and analytical procedures; we articulate explanatory ideas and evolve theories. Without a theory we would not even be able to find our way home, let alone cope with the rich data of musical experience. Conceptual thought and dynamic theorising can illuminate intuitive experiences without destroying them. In research we look for pattern and meaning among the muddle of data, making theoretical models that have explanatory power, reducing uncertainty. I use the term 'dynamic theorising' to emphasise the provisional nature of *all* theories. For example, when the 1986 article had in its title 'the sequence of musical development', this signified only that we were committed to the idea of studying and describing this sequence of development, not that we had finally and for all time exposed to view 'the' sequence.

Because of the underlying theory of musical knowledge, the implications of this study go beyond the specific activity of children composing. It so happens that British music education offers rich opportunities to observe children composing, an activity in schools not so easily found in many other parts of the world. We were fortunate in being able to choose to investigate composing because any insights in this area shine wide pools of light on how people are thinking musically. As we saw in Chapter 3, there are obvious limitations in asking audience-listeners about their understanding of music, not least that the response has to be in a non-musical way, perhaps in words or using a semantic check-form. Asking people to tell us about their musical responses creates a level of ecological interference that is not so evident when we subject composing to a form of 'product analysis'. Even research into performing has certain limitations in permitting us to scan the range of musical understanding. When composing, we are likely to be making musical judgements over a wider range; for example, we can decide on the actual ordering of the music in time and musical space as well as about the manner of producing sounds and shaping phrases. For these and other reasons analysing the compositions of children seemed a useful way to get into their musical worlds and likely to be a good indicator of more general musical development.

'Composing' in this context is defined very broadly, and includes the briefest spontaneous utterances as well as more sustained and rehearsed invention and takes place when there is some freedom to choose the temporal ordering of music, with or without notational and other forms of performance instruction.

Our first step was to take a small random sample of this large musical output and ask three independent observers – teachers – to listen to a tape-recording containing three items from each of seven children, aged 3 to 9; arranged in random order of course. The age of each child was not disclosed but these judges were asked to estimate the ages of the children from the musical evidence they heard on the tape. One of them found the task daunting but the others – who were both experienced teachers *and* musicians – managed the assignment without too much difficulty. The estimated ages given by these two judges closely fitted the actual age of the children, giving a positive statistical correlation (Swanwick and Tillman 1986). There seemed to be a relationship between age and musical development. However, this correlation with age was much less important for us than the fact that the teachers were actually able to recognise changes in the character of the compositions. They had demonstrated that it appears to be possible to distinguish between different kinds of composition; the question was, on what basis were such judgements being made, what were the criteria? Encouraged by these responses, we boldly proceeded to make our own qualitative judgments about the remaining pieces to see if the compositions could be clustered in a coherent way.

As this analysis of the data began to unfold it became possible to fill out the developmental map. The two of us were eventually able to 'place' each of the compositions by the highest observable strand of musical knowledge: materials, expression or form. We also began to see evidence of the development of 'value', an awareness of the significance of music as a substantive part of life. In clustering the compositions into manageable groups of data (Miles and Huberman 1984) we were helped by previous categorisations made by Robert Bunting, based on his own teaching experience (Bunting 1977).

Each of the four layers of musical knowledge eventually came to be seen as encompassing a polarity between 'assimilatory' and 'accommodatory' tendencies. These terms are employed somewhat technically by Piaget, but the concepts are part of our daily experience and it is in that sense that I am using them. The growth of all understanding depends on two complementary and interactive processes: of being able to relate experiential data to our internal systems of meaning (assimilating to our schemata), but also being able to modify these systems when they cease to be adequate to interpret experience and sustain coherence (accommodation). But we have seen this dynamic relationship in action already. Taking things as we first find them – assimilating them directly to our view of the world – is what I have been calling an intuitive process. The refurbishment of these interpretative structures – accommodation – is fundamentally analytical.

This view is not entirely in accord with that of Piaget, who took a rather different position on what he called intuition. My position is that the growth of knowledge at any level emerges intuitively and is nourished and channelled by analysis. Musical knowledge is no exception and observing and participating in the music-making of children offers us further insights into these structures and processes.

On the left-hand side is the playful dimension of internal motivation; starting with the almost entirely intuitive exploration of the sensory qualities of sound, which are transformed into personal expressiveness, then into structural speculation, and ultimately a personal commitment to the symbolic significance of music.

These intuitive insights are extended and nourished by the right-hand side, imitative in its bias and analytical: skill mastery, the conventions of the musical vernacular, idiomatic authenticity, the systematic extension of musical possibilities. Visual representation therefore requires the form of a spiral – or perhaps more accurately, a helix. This can now be seen in relation to the intuitive/analytical dialectic, and we can now add to our concept clusters the ideas of play and imitation and the mighty pair, *assimilation* and *accommodation* (Figure 8).

Having embarked earlier on the development of what might be called a logical model of musical knowledge, we are now faced with the greater complexity of a *psychological* model, a detailed analysis that more adequately represents the dialectical nature of musical engagement. Things do

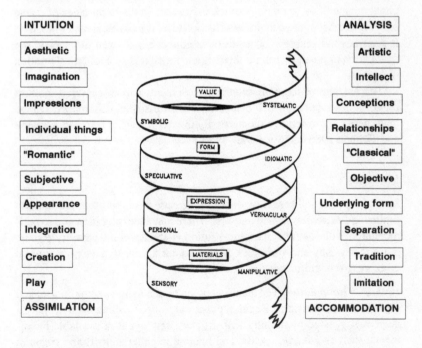

INTUITION	ANALYSIS
Aesthetic	Artistic
Imagination	Intellect
Impressions	Conceptions
Individual things	Relationships
"Romantic"	"Classical"
Subjective	Objective
Appearance	Underlying form
Integration	Separation
Creation	Tradition
Play	Imitation
ASSIMILATION	ACCOMMODATION

VALUE · SYSTEMATIC · SYMBOLIC
FORM · IDIOMATIC · SPECULATIVE
EXPRESSION · VERNACULAR · PERSONAL
MATERIALS · MANIPULATIVE · SENSORY

Figure 8   The left and right of the spiral
Note: The terms 'Romantic' and 'Classical' are here still being used in the special sense developed by Robert Pirsig, as are those provocative words 'subjective' and 'objective'.

seem to get rather technical but I will try to be as clear as I can. Each of the main modes or phases of the developmental spiral is a distinctive shift; they are not simply more of the same thing – quantitative – but are differentially *qualitative*. Into the intuitive, impulsive, initial delight in playing with, exploring and responding to sounds grows the corresponding analytical dimension, an inclination to control sounds, to manipulate, to imitate, to accommodate. With sounds coming under control, musical expression becomes possible; at first intuitively spontaneous but then more conventional, more analytical; accommodating the vernacular commonplaces of phrase and sequence, of metric organisation into common groupings. And these conventional ideas are swept up, assimilated, into an imaginatively playful world of twists of expectation and surprises, intuitive responses to musical form, which may in turn be integrated into the complex frameworks of expectation built up by specific styles or idioms. Beyond this lies the world of recognised symbolic value for the individual and possibly a systematic commitment. To avoid any misunderstanding here about the idea of 'value', it has to be clear that we can enjoy music at any age or level of engagement. 'Valuing' as I am using the term here is more than enjoyment, it points to the phenomenon of us becoming consciously aware of the importance of music as symbolic discourse, a major benefaction to us as individuals and to society. It goes beyond sensory and expressive enjoyment or even pleasure in the fascination of music's structural twists and turns: it is an explicit celebration of 'quality'.

The essence of these developmental elements can be captured in short criterion descriptions which characterise their essential differences. (I give them here only to remove the necessity to refer to earlier texts – Swanwick and Tillman 1986 and Swanwick 1988.)

Materials

Level 1 – Sensory: There is evidence of pleasure in sound itself, particularly timbre and extremes of loud and soft. There may be exploration and experimentation with instruments. Organisation is spontaneous, possibly erratic, pulse is unsteady and variations of tone colour appear to have no structural or expressive significance.

Level 2 – Manipulative: The handling of instruments shows some control and repetitions are possible. Regular pulse may appear along with technical devices suggested by the physical structure and layout of available instruments, such as *glissandi*, scalic and intervallic patterns, trills and *tremolo*. Compositions tend to be long and repetitive as the composer enjoys the feeling of managing the instrument.

Expression

Level 3 – Personal expressiveness: Expressiveness is apparent in changes of speed and loudness levels. There are signs of elementary phrases – musical gestures – which are not always able to be exactly repeated. There is drama, mood or atmosphere, perhaps with reference to an external 'programmatic' idea. There will be little structural control and the impression is of spontaneity without development of ideas.

Level 4 – The vernacular: Patterns appear – melodic and rhythmic figures that are able to be repeated. Pieces may be quite short and will work within established general musical conventions. Melodic phrases may fall into standard 2, 4 or 8–bar units. Metrical organisation is common along with such devices as syncopation, melodic and rhythmic *ostinati* and sequences. Compositions will be fairly predictable and show influences of other musical experiences: singing, playing and listening.

Form

Level 5 – The speculative: Compositions go beyond the deliberate repetition of patterns. Deviations and surprises occur, though perhaps not fully integrated into the piece. There is expressive characterisation which is subject to experimentation, exploring structural possibilities, seeking to contrast or vary established musical ideas. After establishing certain patterns a frequent device is to introduce a novel ending.

Level 6 – The idiomatic: Structural surprises are integrated into a recognisable style. Contrast and variation take place on the basis of emulated models and clear idiomatic practices, frequently, though not always, drawn from popular musical traditions. Harmonic and instrumental authenticity is important. Answering phrases, call and response, variation by elaboration and contrasting sections are common. Technical, expressive and structural control is demonstrated in longer compositions.

Value

Level 7 – The symbolic: Technical mastery serves musical communication. Attention is focused on formal relationships and expressive character which are fused together in an impressive, coherent and original musical statement. Particular groups of timbres, turns of phrase and harmonic progressions may be developed and given sustained concern. There is a strong sense of personal commitment.

Level 8 – The systematic: Beyond the qualities of the previous level, works may be based on sets of newly generated musical materials, such as scales and note rows, novel systems of harmonic generation, electronically created sounds or computer technology. The possibilities of musical discourse are systematically expanded.

Figure 9 is a short-hand version of this sequence, given here for easier reference.

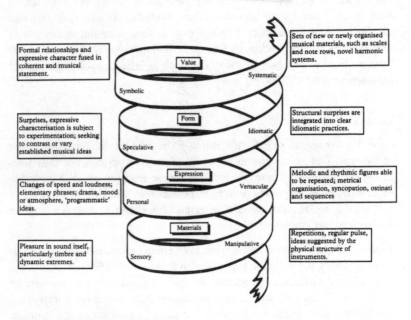

Figure 9   The developmental spiral

There may have been undue attention given to the age-related aspect of this research, though not by us. It was true that – *in general* – the developmental sequence shadowed the age and experience of the children in our particular study. This is hardly surprising. However, this was not the most important aim. We were out to trace the development of musical knowledge in children, not to peg it at precise ages. As we made clear, musical development may follow a certain sequence though not necessarily to a 'standard timetable'. This is important. It is not being suggested that every child at a given age is working at a certain level; far from it. It is very probable that a musically stimulating environment may enhance the levels at which a child may work and the opposite may also be true. And as individuals we move in and out of layers in a fluid way. Although there appears to be a general sequential order, there is wide variation at any particular age, as Figure 10 shows.

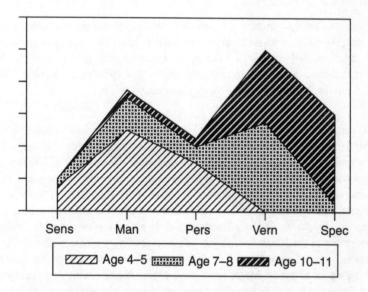

Figure 10 The Swanwick/Tillman data: spiral criteria and age levels

It is not intended to suggest that one layer is somehow better or worse than another but that subsequent phases are more complex than and *include* previous ones. This is an organic model and the process might be compared with the growth of a flower, say a daffodil. We really cannot say that the bloom is more important than the leaves or that these are both more essential than either the stem or bulb. But we can say that – in seasonal growth terms – the bulb becomes active first and the flower appears last and that it is the appearance of the yellow petals that signals the culmination of the growth cycle. Only then may the 'flower' be picked and displayed. It is important to realise that a 'level' is said to be reached when a composition demonstrates the presence of the main characteristics of a level with some consistency, not just a fleeting glimpse. In any event, to avoid a rigid mechanical interpretation of the model, I think it better to substitute the word 'layer' for level and certainly for the rather rigid connotations of 'stage'.

It must be emphasised that there are many musical compositions and performances, effective in their way, that might best be characterised as being essentially in the vernacular, really pastiche; the little military marches by Beethoven for wind bands written in Vienna between two major symphonies (6 and 7), many popular 'musicals' and much 'improvisation' by church organists would be cases in point. Howard Gardner describes what is in essence the vernacular thus.

> ...a reasonably competent 7-years-old should understand the basic metrical properties of his musical system and the appropriate scales, harmonies, cadences, and groupings, even as he should be able, given some motifs, to combine them into a musical unit that is appropriate for his culture, but is not a complete copy of a work previously known.
>
> (Gardner 1973: 197)

It is certainly true that much music is of this kind, and is none the worse for that. There are times when the vernacular is the most appropriate response to a social and musical need. What differentiates the marches of Beethoven from the pieces of a 7-year-old is not their musical level but the place in a productive life which they take and the ease with which the 'professional' knocks them out and indeed can transform the commonplace by giving it a place in a larger design – as Beethoven does with a military march, the last movement of the *Ninth* Symphony. We can also enjoy music within the less intense layers of sound materials and vernacular, depending on the setting in which we are engaged. Music in shops and other public places – such as sport and fitness centres – is usually chosen and inevitably interpreted either on the materials level of a sensory aural environment or in the vernacular mode of the comfortingly familiar. We can listen to *any* music in this way if we choose and depending on the social setting. Music taken at the vernacular level – on my definition – may not necessarily be simple but is felt to be almost entirely predictable; either it has little in the way of structural richness or we are prepared to overlook it.

LOOKING FOR VALIDITY

In her study of children inventing songs, Coral Davies suggests that quite young children demonstrate an understanding of musical structure, especially in the sense of having a beginning, an end and a sense of overall pattern. The conditions for this appear to be encouragement over time and the opportunity to make music vocally, away from the technical demands of instruments. This may indeed be so, though it is difficult to be certain, since most of her examples are of songs where word sounds, patterns and meanings appear to lead the composer-singers into vernacular conventions. These

include regular and answering phrase patterns and sometimes quirky deviations which are so embedded in verbal meanings that it is difficult to isolate
the element of musical speculation. What emerges clearly from this work is
the musical imagery in the minds of very young children. Not so transparent
is whether these expressive icons are organised into speculative relationships
with musical extension, contrast, transformation or surprise. A coherent and
steady image of any kind is in one sense a 'form' – some order having been
brought into the perceptual process. But having an iconic representation, a
mental picture, an internal musical replica, is not necessarily the same as
being able to combine these images in acts of speculation. From recordings
of the music of the children working with Coral Davies it is not always clear
whether or not there is deliberate structural experimentation, 'playing about'
with musical rather than linguistic images.

Davies' research method was to interpret and respond to the songs of
children as 'action research' in the classroom. Since the subsequent evolution
of criteria for composing, it now becomes possible to objectify this approach
a little more by having other people interpret the compositions of her
children. In the arts this idea of inter-subjective judgement is important; it is
the equivalent of a repeated litmus test, the judgement of several people rather
than one individual. In this case, five observers independently listened to the
first 12 of the compositions on the Davies tape. How did these judges perceive
them in the light of the criteria given above, criteria to which Coral Davies

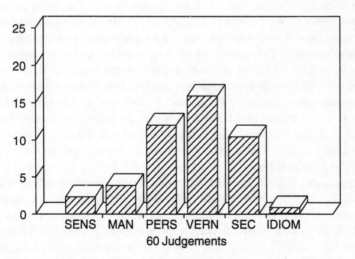

Figure 11 Vocal compositions of young children: five judges place 12
compositions

was working? Figure 11 shows that 14 judgements were made at the speculative level and even one at the idiomatic, while 45 are placed in lower categories.

Drawing on the subjective impressions of more than one person helps us to get some purchase here. There is certainly evidence that musical speculation can be perceived in the invented songs of some 5- to 6-year-old children but perhaps not to the extent originally believed. Seventy-five percent of 60 judgements suggest otherwise. As in language development, adults often impute higher levels of communicative intention than may be steadily in the mind of a child. Our interpretation may be very different from their experience. For instance, just now I am listening to the children in the next-door garden playing. A 7-year-old is leaning out of the window shouting to his 5-year-old brother: 'what are you doing out there?' A third child, aged perhaps between a year and 18 months, also shouts in a parody of the same accentuated tone of voice but is completely unintelligible in terms of verbal meaning. He has picked up the sound shape of his older brother's call but he is not really saying 'what are you doing out there?' nor does he expect an answer. Bruner calls this 'a kind of prosodic envelope' (Bruner 1975).

But 'there is something more that leads the child towards elaborating rule structures in communication'. This 'something more' is that 'play has the effect of drawing the child's attention to communication itself, and to the structure of the acts in which communication is taking place' (p. 10). Play in terms of musical speculation is precisely this enjoyment of musical action which goes beyond making sonorous patterns or expressive gestures. Children elaborate in music, 'searching for varied orders of combining acts and signals' (p. 11). We move beyond imitation into structural experimentation, literally playing with musical ideas, combining expressive gestures into structural patterns that have the potential for surprising and delighting us. We can learn from studies of language acquisition just how important it is to respond to children in ways that affirm the existence of meaning, even if their utterance is not completely formed and crystal clear. So we might respond to the youngest child in the garden as though he had indeed shouted 'what are you doing out there?' with 'mind your own business' and to young composers as though there were indeed speculative ideas in their music: and one day there may be.

As parents or teachers, in the interests of encouraging children's development we tend to assume the highest possible level of intention in the way we *respond*, while at the same time being cautiously realistic in the way we *assess*. It would be unwise to believe that the young child really did understand the linguistic significance of 'what are you doing out there?' and to proceed on that basis at a time of crisis. When a 7-year-old tells me that he has no money because his mother makes him pay half the mortgage, I might respond by commiserating with him but I am not obliged to interpret him literally. That would be a foolish assessment of the situation. He is just talking like a grown up within an 'envelope' of adult manners. In the same way a teacher might respond to the compositions of children in a way that assumes the presence of structural speculation or that they have valued symbolic meaning, in this way anticipating future development.

But does the model describe the data in ways that are true to musical development and does it really relate to Piaget's psychological work? The crucial point here is that we have a possibly helpful way of describing where a composition stands in terms of musical knowledge. The spiral categories go beyond describing levels of skill, though these are included. Manipulative control, the management of the vernacular, idiomatic authenticity; these all say something about musical craft passed on between people and generations, social sharing. But opposite, on the left, are the intuitive mysteries of music: the felt magic of sonorities, the potent sense of the possibilities of expression, the delight of musical form as it leads us as persons on into new relationships.

It needs to be emphasised that this process is not a 'once in a lifetime' affair. The broken ends of the helix indicate that it is constantly being reactivated, as when, for example, we encounter music that is totally new for us or when we have not engaged in music for a long period of time. I once experienced nearly six weeks without hearing or playing music at all. When I finally did come across music it was part of Mendelssohn's *Hebrides Overture* played on a small radio some distance away. The effect of this was like the effect of the sun on the prisoners in *Fidelio* coming up from the dungeons; I was awash with sound materials.

If I am seated at a computer to make music it takes some time before I have explored possible sonorities and learned to control them. For a while I am back at the level of materials. We never leave the earlier levels behind; they are part of the fabric of musical understanding. The point about the longer term developmental sequence is that any educational endeavour should be organised in a way that is relevant to the range of experience and maturation. *In general*, children at the age of 5 to 8 do not aspire to idiomatic authenticity but are entering the world of music with a sense of excitement over sound materials and a willingness to engage with vernacular conventions. *In general*, the story is very different by the age of 14 or so, where making music in 'grown up' idiomatic ways is becoming a strong imperative.

No theoretical framework can explain or explain away any potentially profound experience. The magic remains. But we can become more aware of the fibre that constitutes these experiences. The analysis depicted in the spiral offers the possibility of increasing our awareness of 'what is on' in music and music education and helps to keep the richness of musical knowledge in mind. To take just one issue, when in Britain in the 1970s and following the lead of some contemporary composers, many general music class teachers began again from the source of music – sound itself, they were emphasising the bottom left-hand side of the helix. The next level on the left was also thought important and the phrase 'self-expression' catches an emphasis of that period as does the idea that children should be encouraged to be imaginative, to speculate in music. At the same time – and often in the next room – the instrumental teacher was trying to take students up the right-hand side. But it is not possible to proceed up one side or the other, to rely only on either intuition or analysis. Crossing over from left to right is what children seem to be doing in their own work and this dialectic needs to be respected at all levels of music education. Simply intuitively 'experimenting' and being expressive – 'doing our own thing' – is not sufficient for further musical development; nor is a detached analytical grind in the acquisition of manipulative skills, the ability to work in the vernacular of regular phrases and common metres or even aspiring to stylistic authenticity by simply copying.

Worries about this kind of analysis often seem to focus on the fear of mechanising any understanding of musical response and stereotyping the ways in which we construe and interpret the work of students. The crucial thing though is that this map is organised around the elements of musical knowledge, the four dimensions of critical appraisal: sensitivity to and control of sound materials, of expressive character, of structural relationships, of the recognised value of the experience. The descriptions of the eight elements of the spiral are grouped around these musically validating concepts, and these are based on the centrally important strands of musical knowing.

The mapping of the developmental spiral onto Piagetian concepts raises questions of psychological validity or at least of consistency. To what extent is musical development as I have described it analogous to the general development of mind that is articulated in the theories of Piaget and can we trace parallel concepts throughout the developmental spiral?[1] From early childhood there is an inevitable interaction of accommodation and assimilation – of imitation and play. They do not exist independently, except perhaps fleetingly. It is possible to see very young children engrossed in experimenting with sounds, playfully assimilating them to private worlds, as Piaget puts it, 'a preoccupation with individual satisfaction', enjoying 'the functional pleasure of use' (Piaget 1951: 87–9). But as soon as a child can repeat a musical phrase or the most simple rhythm (in the manipulative mode), accommodation is at work; for however fitful or unsteady that repetition may be, it is made possible by an act of imitation. Even if a repetition immediately follows a model there has to be a guiding internal image, however draft-like and ephemeral, without which we would not be able to reproduce what we heard, not even the shortest pattern.

Together, assimilation and accommodation are at work generating 'sensory-motor intelligence' and, as we saw in Part I, it is this facility of image-making that bridges sensation and thought, making possible the further development of mind. But in the earliest developmental layer – that of musical materials – the fleeting image is locked fairly tightly into the immediate management of sounds.

A qualitative shift is necessary for us to regard music as having a potential for meaning that is metaphorical rather than a direct imitation of sensory phenomena. This transformation is the development of what Piaget calls 'representational imitation', the 'representation of an absent object' (Piaget 1951: 111). Representative imitation lies at the root of musical expressiveness. To produce or empathise with expressive character is essentially to imitate elements of perceived feeling qualities, abstracting them from 'life' and transforming them into gestures.

Such a response to music is not dissimilar from identification of or with a character in a play or film; a musical passage can be heard to dance or languish, it can be expansive or contractive, forwardly impelling or dragging back, angular or flowing, and we may feel ourselves taking on something of these characteristics. We can certainly describe them. As the critic who was writing of a performance of the Brahms violin concerto said, 'it was a genial giant who emerged, refreshed and lighter of heart, in the finale': only a figure of speech of course, but one to which we can surely relate.

Children's music-making in the expressive layer thus moves towards a steadier representation of something that is absent and seems initially to be strongly influenced by visual recollections or verbal suggestions of affective states – hence the easy domination of word-meanings in their invented songs. The first phase of musical expression is an imaginative leap into seeing the possibility of representing life experience in music. The impulse is on the intuitive side – as it always is; intuition is the leading edge and musical expression is at first 'personal', owing little to external models, strongly assimilatory. But this is quickly followed by a tendency to accommodate to vernacular patterns and conventions 'out there' in the environment of musical discourse. Representation passes quickly from fairly spontaneous or 'personal' assimilative activity to the stylisation of these otherwise fleeting shadows, a sign of the growing 'collective rule'.

The development of an understanding of musical structure I supposed to be analogous to what I have called imaginative play – play with images – where expressive characterisations are brought into new relationships and enjoyed as form. To avoid confusion I now think it best to drop the somewhat ambiguous term 'imaginative play' and substitute 'constructional play'. The creative imagination which brought musical expression into being now surfaces intuitively 'in the form of constructions' (Piaget 1951: 87). This is a second qualitative shift to a new level of organisation where musical gestures – phrases, motifs – are assembled into sequential or contrapuntal events. When engaged in musical performance, by matching or contrasting articulation or pointing up similarities or differences between phrases or passages, we are engaged in organising and energising structural groupings and coherence. This aspect of musical inventiveness goes beyond imitatively engaging in expressive characterisation and is transformed into imaginatively playful actions; equivalent to weaving characters into a story, combining single gestures or longer passages into dynamic structural events. Of course, constructional play pre-supposes imitation; we cannot combine non-existent gestures into interactive configurations.

The speculative element crucial to musical form thus has an assimilatory, intuitive bias, obvious in the music-making of children as they search for surprises, creating musical twists and variations. The creation of new juxtapositions seems to be a priority. Once again we set off intuitively; the effectiveness of musical form is evaluated by its capacity to engage, to surprise, to lead the listener on, to explore interactive combinations. Here, constructional play is prime and fairly quickly comes to take place within acceptable idiomatic conventions, the distinctive 'games' developed within the rule frameworks of particular musical styles.

To put this as briefly as I can: each musical development layer represents a *qualitative* shift from sensory engagement, to reproductive imitation, to constructional play. No layer is ever left behind, the processes are taken forward as part of the evolving repertoire of musical intelligence. In every layer there is a dialectic between assimilation and accommodation, a kind of alternating current between intuition and analysis, with intuition leading the way. Musical discourse at any level depends upon the fusion of both sides and when we perceive a perfect equilibrium we speak of 'perfection', of 'quality'. And this 'quality' can be achieved by any person in any layer, though music that has an enduring appeal – perhaps over centuries – will have the potential for interpretation by performers and listeners in *all* layers.

CHECKING FOR RELIABILITY

There are aspects of the original research method that are fairly obviously problematic. Specifically, it could be asked whether the assessment process by which the data were interpreted was really adequate. We chose to make the majority of judgements on the developmental level of the compositions ourselves without an extensive use of independent judges, a form of 'product analysis' that could be said to lack objectivity. There are also questions about the sample of children: for instance, could these findings be repeated in another culture? There were worries too about the thinness of data from older children. For these and other reasons, replication of the original study became essential and the research trail led to an investigation in a different cultural setting, Cyprus.

The music curriculum in Cyprus schools is in process of positive development, with much encouragement being given by Michael Stavrides and his colleagues to the development of composing in the classroom. This work is still relatively recently begun and lacks the history of established practices, such as those promoted elsewhere by various curriculum development projects and endorsed particularly in Britain by the assessment requirements of the 16-plus General Certificate of Secondary Education examination (GCSE) and the legally binding National Curriculum. However, there is very developed work in some Cyprus schools and a number of curriculum activities have been devised with composing as an essential element. It was possible to draw on this work during 1990 to assist in replicating crucial aspects of the earlier London study, testing the reliability of the criteria and, to some extent, the validity of the theoretical model underpinning the developmental spiral.[2]

There were three Cyprus music curriculum projects. These were based on the materials of pentatonic scales, drones and the idea of 'contrast'. We decided to investigate in particular the musical outcomes of the 'contrasts' project, mainly because the idea can be handled by even the youngest children, who might find scales and drones problematic. 'Contrasts' can be interpreted at any level, from materials to form. Twelve teachers in kindergarten, primary and secondary schools were involved and the children worked for three sessions on their pieces. In the third session the compositions were recorded. Over 600 recordings were collected and from these 28 were selected at random. The only sorting rule was that there should be seven items from each of four age groups: 4/5; 7/8; 10/11; 14/15. These 28 items were then assembled in random order on one cassette tape. This may sound a little 'clinical' but we were looking for greater procedural rigour than in the previous London study and wanted to be sure that this particular 'product analysis' was carried out without obvious bias.

This taped sample of 28 compositions was later played to seven primary and secondary music teachers in Britain. They were first given time to study the criterion statements and then were asked to assess the Cyprus compositions, placing each into a criterion category. They were *not* asked to identify the ages of the children but to assign each of the 28 compositions to one of the criterion statements given above.

These teacher-judges were told only of the 'contrasts' project starting point and of the Cypriot origins of the recordings. All judgments were made quite independently by each individual without discussion, usually after one hearing – unless a second hearing was requested. Time was allowed between each item for reflection on the composition and to consider the criterion statements.[3]

The relationship between the actual ages of the children and the placing of compositions by the spiral criteria was analysed and found to be statistically significant.[4] There was a clear ascending relationship, between age and the order of the criteria abstracted from the phases of the spiral. The sequence of developmental levels we originally mapped is reasonably accurate and it follows that the overall theoretical framework has predictive power.

Figure 12 shows the proportion of the 196 judgements made in each of the spiral categories at each age level. It can be seen that the spiral modes arrive on cue and exactly in the predicted sequence. The Sensory, Manipulative and Personal Expression levels are already in place by age 4/5; by age 7/8 the Vernacular is established; by 10/11 the Speculative appears; and compositions at age 14/15 show the first emergence of the Symbolic mode.

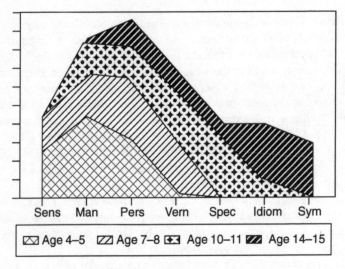

Figure 12 Cyprus data: spiral criteria and age levels

Differences between the data

There is one apparent difference that can be easily observed by inspection of the two sets of data. This prediction was originally signalled thus.

> We suspect that, if children are in an environment where there are musical encounters, then this sequence may be followed more quickly. The

opposite may also, unfortunately, be true: in an impoverished environment, development is likely to be minimal, arrested.

(Swanwick and Tillman 1986: 338)

Children in Cyprus schools are certainly not in an impoverished musical environment but there is unquestionably less of a tradition of composing in the classroom. We were also assessing compositions from several Cyprus schools where children had different teachers, unlike earlier data-gathering in Britain, where one teacher was systematically engaged in developing a rich musical curriculum during the four-year period of the research. We might therefore expect more variability in the Cyprus compositions and possible lower levels of achievement as assessed by the criteria. For example, among the UK children we could anticipate more confidence with the musical vernacular and greater fluency in structural speculation with a greater dispersion of the lower criterion levels in the higher age groups among the Cyprus sample. An inspection of the data suggests this may be so. By analysis we can determine that, although the sequential order of development may be identical, the compositions of the UK children appear generally to be more advanced than those of their Cyprus peers and that there is greater variance among the Cypriot children.[5]

This evidence gives credence to the structure of the original music developmental map and fulfills the projections made for the older age group. Furthermore, in the light of the differences between the two samples it is tempting provisionally to hypothesise that music education in schools is able to make a difference to the musical development of children. However, the research was not designed to test this and it would be unwise to rely on these results to support what would be, for music educators, an attractive thesis.

Several questions are raised by these findings and further work would be helpful. A comment by one of the British teacher-judges was to the effect that the criterion statements would be an improvement on some current ways of assessing children's compositions. There is indeed a need and some potential here for developing more reliable, more musically valid and cross-cultural assessment techniques and the necessity of sensitising judges responsible for the assessment of musical compositions. In music education there is a central problem of how we validly assess the music-making and music-taking of ourselves and others. How do we become sensitive critics? Can what we learn from studying children's composing be applied to other musical activities – to performance and audience-listening? It is to the processes of assessment along a wider front that the research trail now leads us, not to satisfy the clamour for public accountability but to better understand the nature of transactions in music and music education and therefore to be able to respond more appropriately to the music-making and musical responses of students and others who may be engaged in music.

6   Assessing musical knowledge

IMPROVING ASSESSMENT

Every teacher assesses; assessment is an integral part of teaching, for in order to respond helpfully to students we are necessarily forming and articulating impressions of what characterises their work. These appraisals have their origin in intuition but they have to be developed further if we are to avoid being arbitrary, basing any judgement on the whim of the moment. Assessment should be founded on some considered idea of what is at issue, what is central in the particular subject or activity. In the case of music we have to know what counts when people perform, compose or respond to music as audience-listeners. It is unacceptable to rely only on how we happen to be feeling at the time, especially if for any reason we are not able to respond sympathetically to the work of a particular student. If there is to be any meaningful interaction between teacher and student in schools and colleges, hidden assumptions underlying assessment have to be brought out into the light. It is not necessary for this transaction to be short-handed into a grade, nor need it be comprehensive. But there must be a sense of what really matters, an attitude of focused critical judgement. Intuitive responses are sustained and developed by appropriate analysis.

Beyond these informal but inevitable day-to-day assessments in which all teachers and students are involved, lies the more contentious area of public assessment, reporting judgements to others – parents, college entry committees, potential employers. Usually this requires verbal descriptions, marks, grades, or perhaps a ranking order list. These formal assessments are intended to place the work of the student either by comparison with others (norm referencing) or in relation to criteria implicit within the activity itself (criterion referencing). The difference here is important. Assessing people in order to select the tallest 20 percent or the 10 percent with the highest IQ scores or marks on a music ability test would be norm-referenced selection. Alternatively, the car driving test or a graded examination in music are examples of criterion referencing where we have to meet specific requirements to do with handling a vehicle, safe driving, fluency on an instrument, interpretation and so on.

Assessment by declared criteria has permeated all educational systems, though the very idea of criteria may be viewed with suspicion by some of those working in the arts. It may be thought that the muses are too unique and personal to yield to the crudities of grading and marks or matched to a criterion statement and that we should assess the 'process' and not the 'product'. We ought immediately to dispose of this unnecessary dualism and certainly avoid slipping the word 'end' in before 'product'. Products are simply the things we make or say at any time and processes are totally invisible, inaudible without products. To observe anything of the actual conceptual and feeling processes of any individual would require us to study a wide range of his or her products on frequent occasions. Even then it would seem presumptuous to believe that we have either the right, the sensitivity or the knowledge to comprehend personal processes, though we might become more confident over seeing the direction in which the work appears to be leading. Essentially we assess those things that are produced by students and it is less ambitious and more honest to concede that it is usually the *work* we assess and not individual *persons*. When I am inclined to describe the little military marches that Beethoven wrote around 1810 as being in the 'vernacular' this is not a comment about Beethoven in general but about this particular corner of his work.

Once we accept this important limitation it is possible to become more objective about assessment processes. In any art there may be major outcomes beyond the reach of any form of assessment. Perhaps the most significant learning experiences are always tacit, unspeakable, incommunicable and therefore out of range of assessment. We certainly have to know when to stand back and refrain from rushing into judgements and interpretations, for to do so insensitively is an intrusion. But this is not to say that music is totally indefinable, that musical knowledge is an absolute mystery and that teachers have nothing to say about what students do. We can develop as sensitive critics, leaving many things unsaid but intuitively focusing on those things that seem especially important. We also need to analyse what appears to be happening as a process over time, as we can see from the following extract from a case study of young people composing.

This is an effective piece; yet it seems inconsistent with the rest of Celina's work. The use of 'ad lib' passages, syncopation and irregular metre are familiar – but where are the restless energy, the intensity, the exploration of scales and tonality? Instead we have a stylised coolness. This may reflect a new facet of Celina's character; for the first time we find her thinking harmonically, both introduction and main section being based on chord sequences. Or it may be that she did not feel able to push herself to the limit – she was certainly under great pressure from the demands of other work and her commitments as a performer. But if this is a makeweight, it is still the work of a powerful musical intelligence.

(Bunting 1988: 305)

This reflection on the musical products of one person as they appear to change over time goes beyond the intuitive and includes an attempt to account for these changes, to give reasons. There is no escaping analysis and interpretation. As Robert Bunting tells us, 'I must to some extent select, omit and simplify, and the way I do this must betray a personal point of view' (p. 269). Once again we see the inescapable interaction between intuition and analysis and if it were possible always to give this amount of care and attention to each pupil and his or her work we would indeed be in an ideal educational situation. Unfortunately we are not. In one school where I worked for four years I saw over 650 different students each week in scheduled classes, in addition to directing two choirs (one of which performed in three parts daily in school assembly), two orchestras and facilitating three jazz groups and other ensembles.

Many music teachers work in similar settings, especially in secondary or high schools. Assessment under such conditions can rarely reach such levels of detail and specificity. When it does it is seldom possible to report in meticulous detail to those who were not present during the transactions, whether they are parents, headteachers or the readers of a journal. Assessment is part of the very fabric of teaching but inevitably gets condensed, coded and often distorted by institutional pressures. Such case studies as those described by Robert Bunting serve to remind us of the complexity of music-making processes and of the individuality of each student. They also hold before us the vision of an educational setting, where time and small student numbers are conducive to observing and reporting in a way that maintains intuitive integrity yet, at the same time, encourages sensitive analysis and lively theorising. Unfortunately we are frequently required to assess the work of students without the luxury of ample time and are obliged to give an account to outsiders in ways that are understandable.

Whatever reservations we may have about the limitations and dangers of formalised assessment, the public adjudication of music is a very common-place event. We notice it most conspicuously in musical performance, especially in graded examinations, at festivals and in national and international competitions. Yet the validity and reliability of the processes by which these judgements are made seems largely unquestioned, even though fair comparisons may be quite hard to substantiate; as when performers play different pieces at varying levels of technical difficulty on dissimilar instruments but are still assessed in comparison with one another. In spite of such impediments, assessment of musical performance during competitions and examinations can be quite crucial for the performer and judgements may enhance or diminish personal status or career expectations and even lead to financial loss or gain.

I have tried to show how valid criterion statements can be developed that facilitate the assessment of children's compositions and which stem from studies of children composing. These criteria have been found practically helpful by teachers and can also facilitate research across into the development of musical knowledge. Looking back at the description by Robert Bunting of the work of Celina we can see that it seems to match the criterion of the 'idiomatic' and listening to the work itself confirms this impression. The performance is indeed stylised but 'lacking the restless energy, the intensity' that might suggest the 'symbolic' mode as described on p. 89.

> Structural surprises are integrated into a recognisable style. Contrast and variation take place on the basis of emulated models and clear idiomatic practices, frequently, though not always drawn from popular musical traditions. Harmonic and instrumental authenticity is important. Answering phrases, call and response, variation by elaboration and contrasting sections are common. Technical, expressive and structural control is demonstrated in longer compositions.

We might also notice that the introductory passage has more of the feeling of the commonplaces of the 'vernacular' about it, and that it is not until the entry of the saxophone – played by Celina's uncle – that the music swings into a confident idiom. The question as to who is the real composer here is not very important, unless we are constrained to give a grade.

Valid assessment criteria must be true to the essential nature of musical knowledge, at the same time recognising the need for economy of time that is imperative in most classroom transactions, where a music teacher may be working with hundreds of individuals every week. Desirability has to come to terms with feasibility. It is possible to employ criterion statements to get some kind of grasp on the musical work of students without trivialising or misrepresenting either music or the intentions of the student. The first requirement is to acknowledge the complexity of musical experience itself.

Clearly such a rich activity cannot be reduced to just a single dimension, say that of 'technique'. There are the other recognised elements, including whatever is sometimes called 'musicality', which we can more clearly identify as sensitivity to and control of materials, expression and form. On the other hand, it seems inappropriate to identify several dimensions and give some kind of judgement on each of these separately. This sometimes happens; for example in ice skating, where separate sets of marks may be given for technique and artistry, marks which are then summed and averaged. In music one might do the same. There are in the British GCSE examination system procedures for assessing children's compositions which consist of giving marks in different categories: melody, harmony, texture, overall and so on, adding them up to get a single figure.[1] The conflation into a single figure of two or more observations hardly seems to be very meaningful assessment and loses important information on the way. For instance, in competitive ice skating a performer might be given 6 out of 10 for technique and 9 for artistry, while another contender gets 9 for technique and only 6 for artistry. The sum of each set of marks happens to be the same – 15 – but the impression of the performances will be quite different. The fudge of adding a marking category called 'overall' only makes things worse. It suggests that, although a reductive analysis has been made of the essential dimensions of the activity, it is unreliable and we therefore need to fall back on a global intuitive impression. When in doubt this is always wise, but unfortunately in this particular situation intuition and analysis are not integrated within the judgement but separated out. They may even be in conflict.

We have to resist relegating criterion-based judgements to the poor levels of meaning embodied in numerical marks and contest the spurious impression these numbers may give of more or less exact quantification. This is obvious in music where, for example, we might find it hard to assess the relative degree of potential technical difficulty between two pieces. It is possible to get round this by specifying levels of technical difficulty and limiting the highest levels of achievement to the most difficult category. For instance, we might say that playing a simple slow melody based on a few adjacent notes is easier than managing a wide span of leaping notes that have to be delivered with some velocity. Surely the person playing the 'easy' piece ought not to get such high marks as the other one? This is not totally satisfactory and may make too much of relative virtuosity, as well as luring performers into water technically too deep for the good of their musical development. There is a further problem if we attempt to equate the technical levels of, say, a piano performance of a Chopin *Mazurka*, a Scott Joplin *Rag* and a Bach *Fugue*. On the surface (though depending on the actual pieces) these may appear to be similar in difficulty; they are often grouped together in examination syllabuses.

There are different *kinds* of technical challenge here, not simply of a quantitative order. While Bach requires clear and balanced part-playing with matching articulation for each appearance of the same material, Chopin and Joplin need an accurately leaping left hand and careful colouring of the chords in the inside parts that does not detract from the elaborate flow of melody above. It might be hard to say which piece is the most demanding to play; there are different difficulties. Yet we can say something meaningful about the level of skill and musicianship of a pianist playing one piece and someone else playing another; in the same way that it is possible to say of a well-known tennis player, an Olympic high-jumper and an international footballer that they are *all* fine athletes. We do this by applying general criteria that define what it means to be athletic; there is a *quality* that we recognise as musical. The problem is to define this quality in a way that provides reasonably explicit grounds for judgement and at the same time remains true to music; issues of reliability and validity.

QUALITATIVE CRITERIA

It is for these reasons that criterion statements have become common in education at every level and in all areas of the school and college curriculum. Criterion statements may appear to be potentially fair and relatively easy to use but they require to be carefully devised, hierarchically sequential and their function clearly understood. Relating an event to a criterion statement is like matching our impression of someone to an 'identikit' picture used by the police; 'yes', we say, 'she was more like this than like that' and this is basically a holistic, intuitive judgement. The picture may be initially made up from an analysis of different elements but we are asked to see it whole. In the same way we cannot use just a part of a criterion statement; either there is a fairly good match or there is not. When using these criteria in musical assessment, a composition or performance is seen to match a particular *qualitative* category – the little Beethoven marches essentially have the quality of the vernacular. Any manageable and reliable form of criterion assessment is essentially dependent on the recognition of the qualitative, not on numerical quantity.

Criterion statements then should themselves meet certain prerequisites.

(a) they should be clear;
(b) they should be qualitatively different from each other;
(c) they should be brief enough to be quickly understood but substantial enough to be meaningful;
(d) they should be able to be hierarchically ordered in a clear and justifiable sequence;
(e) they should be useful in a range of settings, including different achievement levels and musical styles;
(f) they should reflect the essential nature of the activity – in our case they should be true to the nature of music.

The last of these is paramount. Musical assessment is not a free-for-all. If 'anything goes' it would be very difficult to justify music as an element of any curriculum and impossible to believe in a fair or meaningful system of assessment, for there would be no basis for any kind of critical judgement. Intuition – as always – has to be tempered by analytical explication, in the same way that the left-hand side of the developmental spiral cannot be sustained without the right.

JUDGING PERFORMANCES

I have already put forward criteria for assessing the musical compositions of students, statements that are based on the layers of musical understanding. These have been shown fairly reliably at work in different situations. Similar criteria have also been found helpful in the assessment of musical perform-ances, statements that describe levels of music-making by reference to the major elements of musical experience: sound materials, expressive charac-terisation, structural sequencing, valuing. As with composing, the musical validity of this enterprise depends on the comprehensive nature of these elements, a philosophical problem at the outset. Reliability depends on a high level of inter-personal agreement, both about the criteria themselves and the way in which they attract the agreement of independent observers. This is both a philosophical and an empirical problem and to some extent it has to be tackled in a practical way. The eight criterion statements for composing were therefore redrafted with a slant towards assessing performing. Each was typed on a separate card, not numbered or labelled in any way and the set of eight shuffled into random order. Working in nine groups of three or four people, 30 experienced music teachers ordered the cards into what seemed to be the most likely succession, running from the statement reflecting the lowest level of performance to that signifying the highest.

There was a very high level of agreement within and between the nine groups of judges concerning the likely hierarchical order of the statements. It was possible for them to place the cards in a generally agreed order, thus suggesting that the statements were indeed clear and qualitatively differen-tiated from each other and that they could be quickly understood, meaningful and were able to be hierarchically ordered into a sequence.[2] Minor changes in some statements were made, mainly in an attempt to remove confusion between levels two and three, a possibility that had been identified by the teachers in subsequent discussion. This fine-tuned version is given below with the level numbers added.

Criterion cards – musical performance : final version

Level 1: The rendering is erratic and inconsistent. Forward movement is unsteady and variations of tone colour or loudness appear to have neither structural nor expressive significance.

Level 2: Control is shown by steady speeds and consistency in repeating patterns. Managing the instrument is the main priority and there is no evidence of expressive shaping or structural organisation.

Level 3: Expressiveness is evident in the choice of speed and loudness levels but the general impression is of an impulsive and unplanned performance lacking structural organisation.

Level 4: The performance is tidy and conventionally expressive. Melodic and rhythmic patterns are repeated with matching articulation and the interpretation is fairly predictable.

Level 5: A secure and expressive performance contains some imaginative touches. Dynamics and phrasing are deliberately contrasted or varied to generate structural interest.

Level 6: There is a developed sense of style and an expressive manner drawn from identifiable musical traditions. Technical, expressive and structural control are consistently demonstrated.

Level 7: The performance demonstrates confident technical mastery and is stylistic and compelling. There is refinement of expressive and structural detail and a sense of personal commitment.

Level 8: Technical mastery totally serves musical communication. Form and expression are fused into a coherent and personal musical statement. New musical insights are imaginatively and systematically explored.

The remaining question is whether they can really be useful in a range of musical performance settings, where there are different achievement levels and various musical styles. Eleven recorded performances which previously had been submitted for a General Certificate of Secondary Education examination were played to seven teacher-judges. The performances included *Domine Deus* by Vivaldi, Beethoven's *Für Elise*, a folk tune played on recorder, an ensemble playing the popular song, *You are Always* and a specially composed piece played on electronic keyboards. Without any discussion and quite independently, the seven judges reached a statistically high level of consensus about the relative merit of the performances, different in kind though they all were.[3] The least reliable judge in terms of agreement with others was the 'real' examiner who had finalised the GCSE marks – the published scores that really count – but this person had not been working to criterion statements.

Since musicians and music educators are required to assess musical performances fairly frequently, we would do well to come clean over our criteria and to look more closely at the perspective of more than one assessor. Otherwise arbitrariness and unexamined bias may cause not only unfairness but may prevent an adequate response to the work of students. Criterion statements are a way of making explicit the basis of our judgements and are also a way of articulating these judgements to others. The following more openly clustered version of the criteria for performance is currently being used to assess the work of students in one college at degree level.

Criteria For Assessing Performance In Higher Education

D Grade (Third class)

The performance is generally tidy and conventionally expressive with matching articulation throughout. There is little evidence of structural awareness or sense of musical development throughout the piece and the course of the music is fairly predictable.

C Grade (Lower second)

A secure and expressive performance contains some imaginative touches. Dynamics, articulation and phrasing are matched, contrasted and varied to generate structural interest and demonstrate relationships between the various musical ideas.

B Grade (Upper second)

There is a developed sense of musical style and a convincing expressive manner drawn from identifiable musical traditions. Contrasted and re-peated material is integrated into a coherent, developing whole and the voice or instrument is handled with reliable sensitivity.

A Grade (First class)

The performance demonstrates confident technical mastery which always serves musical communication. The attention of the listener is focused on structural relationships and expressive character fused in a coherent and original musical statement and there is refinement of expressive and structural detail along with a sense of personal commitment.

Fail Grade

The handling of voice or instrument may show some degree of control though not consistently so and there are numerous technical accidents. Managing the instrument appears to be the main priority and there is little if any expressive shaping or structural cohesion.

The fact that such statements facilitate consensus judgements and appear to help in both informal and formal assessment is encouraging. Furthermore, the transposition between composing and performing suggests that the foundations of the criteria run pretty deep and relate well to the bedrock of musical knowing. However, life is not so simple. The good researcher is not only concerned to argue for a thesis but to try to unsettle it; in Popper's terms, to falsify the theory (Popper 1972). There may be alternative explanations for the high levels of consensus between judges and one of the most likely candidates is simply a numerical scale. If we ask people to assess a musical performance or composition simply using a scale from one to eight, without any attached qualitative description, can they do this reliably with inter-judge consistency?

The same tape of the 28 Cyprus compositions previously used to replicate the original developmental spiral research was played to seven teacher-judges in Cyprus. They all had a university degree in music and were involved in an in-service course at the Pedagogical Institute in Nicosia. These teachers had no previous knowledge of the Swanwick/Tillman criteria and – as with the English teacher-judges – they made judgements independently of each other. The results show high levels of inter-judge agreement, not significantly different from the earlier assessment of the same compositions.[4]

These judges seem just as able to put into rank order the compositions of children on an unlabelled scale from one to eight as they are on a scale attached to eight criterion statements. What are we to make of this? It is certainly possible to hierarchically order both the statements and the compositions independently. For all practical purposes and under certain conditions it might be worth *not* using criterion statements. However, they have value, serving a purpose in analysing and clarifying the bases of intuitive judgements. Although it seems possible for musically and educationally experienced judges to function without criterion statements, this might well become more problematic if only one or two compositions are being assessed in isolation, without the benefit of instant comparison with many others. Criterion statements are a form of analysis not necessarily required when intuitive judgements can be made by sensitive observers. But they appear to have validity and they explicitly expose the grounds for critical judgement without apparent conflict with intuitive assessment.

From the theoretical basis lying behind the formulation of these criteria we have the possibility of understanding more about the generic nature of musical knowledge, those elements that are shared in various settings: composing, performing and audience-listening. The next turn of the research trail takes us in the direction of the audience-listener. Do the same layers of meaning permeate the listening experience? We shall need more than the semantic differential or other limited choice responses to begin to answer this question.

PROBING AUDIENCE-LISTENING

In an extended study carried out by Liane Hentschke in England, we listened to what children had to say about music.[5] Sixty children told us quite a lot. They came from a cross-section of English schools – 20 children selected at random from classes in each of Years 2, 6 and 9 (ages 7/8, 10/11 and 13/14). The research method was a structured interview which allowed some freedom to sequence questions and flexibility in responding to each child. This allows us to explore the range of musical response without too many fixed questions which might distort the conversation and stereotype the answers. However, an interview is a method prone to bias on the part of the researcher. For example, a biased question which might 'lead the witness' would be, 'which instrument is playing?'. Here the invitation is to respond in terms of musical materials. A procedure was therefore devised to minimise the chance of the interviewer leading the children towards certain kinds of answer and at the same time giving more than one opportunity to listen to the music.

In the interview each pupil listened to three pieces of music and after each one chose from four different possibilities a card with a picture of a human figure. These four pictures depicted stick figures in various attitudes of activity or rest. The children were asked, 'which of the cards would you choose to describe the music?'. After choosing a card, each child was invited to write or draw something which may help them remember something about the piece. The students then listened to the same extract a second time, after which more open-ended questions were asked, such as: 'what can you tell me about the music you have listened to?', 'if you had to describe this music to a friend who had never heard this music before, what would you say about it?', 'what kind of things did you notice in the music?'. Other conversation followed, based on the child's comments. For example, if someone said, 'this is classical music' the researcher might ask, 'what makes you think this music is classical music?'. After completing this procedure with the first three musical extracts, each child was asked to listen to all three in sequence without any interruption. After listening, and with the chosen picture cards and any notes or drawings as an aide memoire, the child was asked to choose the 'odd one out' of the three pieces and then say why this choice was made.

This process was repeated with two other groups of three pieces. There was a reason for grouping extracts in clusters of three. We were trying to find out how children construe music and especially if this changes at different ages; the research model here is related to that of the Repertory Grid with origins in Kelly's Personal Construct Theory (Kelly 1955). This technique is described by Fransella and Bannister (1977: 4) as 'a particular form of structured interview' and has been used by different researchers in the field of music education, including Hargreaves (1986), Ward (1986), and Gilbert (1990). The essential procedure is to have people look at or think about three things and decide which two have something in common and which is the 'odd one out'.

In this way and over several choices, a pattern of personal constructs is revealed, showing how the individual views or construes his or her world.

For instance, we might take the elements of mother, uncle, aunt and other 'triads' of relatives. Over a number of such pairings and singling out it may become apparent that the person may be grouping relatives by the construct of gender, or perhaps by age, or by closeness within the family structure, or by geographical proximity.

In our case the musical extracts were chosen according to what appeared to the researcher to be their most striking feature – three sets of three extracts, a total of nine. The first extract in each triad is distinct from the others in terms of sound materials – it has quite different instrumentation. The second extract has a quite different expressive character from the other two, embodied mainly in speed and loudness level. The third extract has a striking structural feature, some clear change takes place. The aim here was to see if children at different ages compared and contrasted music on the basis of materials, expression and form, perhaps with changes at different ages. Obviously, it is difficult to control these variables since all music necessarily embodies all three strands and, as it turned out, the results of this use of the repertory grid were by no means conclusive. Its main virtue appeared to be in helping children to think about the music and to give a focus for their listening for a third time.

Making such choices is yet another instance of musical analysis that does not depend on words. However, the evidence of what the children actually *said* about the nine pieces takes us a little further. Here are some fairly typical examples. (Because of the ages and concentration span of the younger children only the first part of each piece was played.)

1 Chris Rea, *Hired Gun* (Introduction)

7/8 years: piano * nice music

10/11 years: you want to sit down and listen to it * it was played by a piano * relaxing * in-between pop music and classical music, because it's got a nice rhythm but is played on a classical instrument

13/14 years: very slow, relaxing and very sad * most of the music was played by the piano except at the end * harmony played a nice part in the music * very interesting music, you can sit and relax to it, because it is very slow and there are no differences within the music, apart from different loudness at the end

2 Dionne Warwick, *Heartbreaker* (Introduction)

7/8 years: kind of fast * ballet music

10/11 years: good to dance to * nice rhythm * pop music, because it's got a lot of drums in it * I liked it

13/14 years: catchy beat, a very nice piece of music, quite easy to listen to * very bouncy and happy * quite high, bouncy and there is a beat to it at the background, and it seems to be the beginning of a pop tune * it is jazzy, because it was played with a beat by the synthesiser * it had a pop beat to it * it was not classical music because it had a nice tune * it wasn't orchestral

3   Phil Collins, *That's Just the Way It Is* (Introduction)

7/8 years: a pop star would sing this * it was a drum
10/11 years: wooden instruments at the beginning and strings * had a drum beat * the wooden instruments at the beginning had a pattern and later it went faster * relaxing after the percussion instruments
13/14 years: this music makes you feel the music rather than listen to it, because it makes you take notice of what was actually played * very nice and very 'flowy' * the second part was very bouncy and then comes the flowy part * I like this type of music best, because you can feel it, and makes you feel involved in it * sounded like night, but when the drums come in it sounded like stones falling

4   Chopin, *Waltz No. 1 in E♭ Major*, op. 18 (opening)

7/8 years: it is the kind of music people would like to listen to this * kind of relaxing music
10/11 years: I liked the dynamics * I was aware when it got louder and quieter in the music * piano * classical dancing music, because it is from a traditional composer such as Mozart * lively
13/14 years: this is a kind of happy dance music, played just by the piano * very lively * the beginning is slightly different from the rest of the music, giving the impression that it was going to be a different tune, as it was * but the tune is recognisable * it's 'dancy' * flowy and jumpy piece of music and it went together very well * this music sticks in your head, because it was repeated twice, plus it was a jumpy tune that you might not easily forget

5   Dvořák, *Serenade for Strings in E (1st movement – opening)*

7/8 years: played by violin * people would like to dance to this
10/11 years: low, bits went quite fast and then slow * classical because it is played on old instruments and it sounds unlike music we hear today * it sounds different because of the instruments and the way it is played, the rhythm perhaps

13/14 years: this music has a lot of feeling * it paints a picture in your mind, like a forest and as you went through the forest it was quite dark – the lower part of the music – but then it came up to an opening allowing the sun shine through the trees and a stream running down represented by the other part of the music * it was very deep to begin with and slowly goes up and then it stays up high and it did not get down again * I would say to my friends that this music is different from the type they like, that is classical and gives you pictures in your head * it is classical because it is played by the strings and nowadays the music don't paint as many picture in your head any more, only a few artists do that

6   Haydn, *Symphony No. 101 in D, 'The Clock'* (start of the *Andante*)

7/8 years: it is high music * strange sort of music
10/11 years: in the beginning there were 'plucking' cellos * nice to listen to * high sounds * the first bit was dismal
13/14 years: very bouncy, plucky, which gave a bit energy in my head * it sounds like chicken plucking at the ground and perhaps a horse playing a part. It has a very steady beat to it * people like to listen to this kind of music, it is refreshing

7   Debussy, *Suite Bergamasque, Passepied* (opening)

7/8 years: it is fast
10/11 years: short notes which made it sound very fast * piano, dancing music because of the rhythm * sounds like rain drops because of the short notes
13/14 years: it is very fast * it is full of different parts of music, while one goes on there are others on top of that * it makes you feel like the player of the music * it looks like the person is in a rush to do it, very rushy and then it got very loud in the middle and then it went back to the first part * the beat went high and low and above that there was a tune, as though a person was in a rush to do things

8   Elgar, *Introduction and Allegro for Strings* (opening)

7/8 years: it is very loud and kind of resting
10/11 years: really dismal because of the low notes * not to dance to, just good to listen to * low and louder in the beginning and then it went quieter * sad
13/14 years: mainly violins, string instruments * they are all very dramatic * it is the sort of music you have in the films when something

dramatic happens * it causes a dreadful feeling because the way it was playing very low and all of a sudden a high note was playing, which made you feel like something had been discovered, perhaps someone has been shot down

9   Mendelssohn, *Octet in E♭*, op. 20, 4th movement (start)

7/8 years: fast music
10/11 years: dancing music because it was fast * lively, not very loud * string instruments * nice rhythm, you can tap your feet to it
13/14 years: very active, the violins played a fast part in it which slowly built up with different instruments * sounded like the people that played really enjoyed it * it built up quite dramatic because the beat was very fast and did move up quite fast * it was dramatic because some strings – the violins – were playing very low and then going very high and loud and then moving down slowly, and then moving up a bit

We see immediately that the older children had much more to say about all the pieces of music. This is not necessarily that older children talk more – as anyone who spends time with younger children will confirm. By the age of 13 to 14 young people are becoming more analytically aware, more able to articulate something of their musical experience. Here again we can see the dimensions of musical knowledge at work as they talk about music and we can plot these into graphic form by looking at everything said by the 20 children from each of the three age groups. This gives 180 statements from each age level. Taking each individual response as a whole and bearing in mind the developmental and performance criteria, we can look for evidence of the highest level of comment. Some responses stay at the level of descriptions of materials (instruments and so on), others also engage with expressive character (often in terms of pictures or stories), while a few draw our attention not only to materials and expression but also to musical form. Figure 13 shows the distribution.

We can see that these children tend to say things that are confined to sound materials and expressive character most especially at younger ages and that comments which include reference to musical form appear mostly among the oldest group, hardly ever before.[6] It does seem that the development of audience-listening follows the same sequence as the flowering of composing. If this is so we may be on surer ground when with children. They seem to want to talk about expressive character at almost any age, though not about musical form at 6 years old or even sometimes at 10. By the age of 14 they are noticing the relationships inherent in the structure of music. Of course, by then any discussion of music is likely to include *all* layers. Here is an

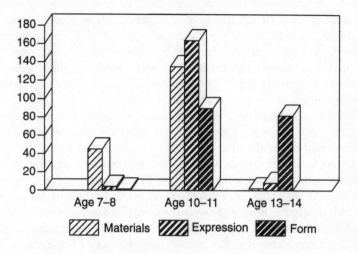

Figure 13 Levels of musical analysis revealed in interview

example from one of the older children which encompasses analysis of materials, expressive character and form. From this description the reader might even be able to identify which piece is in the spotlight.

> It was quite slow – two beats in a bar – and started with a low instrument which played and carried on through the whole piece, playing two beats, which were not the same notes, quite jumpy. On the top of this there were high string instruments playing the main tune, and they were very smooth, and there are quite a few running bits and the notes were 'slowish'. The whole tune is quite quiet and it sounded like a very slow water running, quite sleepy and peaceful.

EDUCATION: A MEETING PLACE FOR INTUITION AND ANALYSIS

Like the composer Birtwhistle, these young people are aware of the extraordinary communicative power of music and are able to say something about it. Words, graphs and other forms of notation can never be a substitute for music directly experienced but they can help to articulate certain facets of meaning which otherwise might escape us altogether. Notations of any kind are forms of representation which serve to shape the particular features of the realities we are trying to construe; they are analytical devices. Whether they be visual signs for music indicating loudness, length, timbre or pitch, or pictures in the form of graphs of how people actually perceive music; notational representations are always secondary to the *presentations* of meaning that must ultimately be grasped intuitively. But words, labels and pictures – notations of our experience – however partial and limited, can help to enrich the ways in which we take the world and are a necessary element of musical and educational discourse.

Education depends upon the development of representational possibilities, of finding images, metaphors, and devising activities which bring out the essential nature of music and enable us to share our perspectives. We ought not to leave it to chance, to society or the media. Although no one can possibly avoid contact with music and intuitive knowledge is open to everyone, music as part of a school curriculum offers the possibility of levels of analysis which can enlarge and deepen intuitive response.

We can see something of the interaction of intuition and analysis in the study by Liane Hentschke. Her research with children in British schools was preceded by a similar work undertaken in Brazil. Brazil has no well-developed national school music curriculum but has instead a general arts programme, which tends to mean that music gets little attention. Musical instruction is usually available only through private teaching and in the special music schools. There are, of course, several cultural differences at work here that differ from the English context, besides the presence or absence of a school music programme. It happens also that the average age of the Brazilian children was about six months younger.

Even so, in spite of the hazards of making comparisons between the groups of children in Brazil and England, there are implications that a music curriculum does have an effect. Figure 14 suggests that the Brazilians had much less to say to Dr Hentschke about music than English students of the same age, and their observations – their musical analyses – were not as richly layered, and this in spite of the fact that the researcher in Brazil was conversing with children in her own language and city.[7]

We might be tempted to put these differences down simply to a reluctance to verbalise about music but this would be a mistake. The Brazilian children were very willing to talk in response to music, often using it as a launching pad for elaborate imaginative stories of their own or to recall specific events in their recent family and social life. Their accounts are certainly coherent but suggest that sound materials or expressive qualities had acted to stimulate anecdotes which very soon led away from the music into other reflections. There was no evidence at all of attention to the structural unfolding of music – even with the older group – and more restricted accounts of changes in levels of expressiveness. And yet there is music-making in the media and on the streets of Brazil, though we need to be careful not to romanticise here.

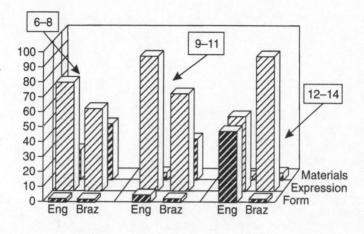

Figure 14 Levels of analysis: children in Brazil and England

Music is not all-pervasive in Brazilian culture, though it is powerfully present for some.

I have argued that intuitive response and analysis are mutually reinforcing energies that together generate musical knowledge. Formal education provides a framework for sensitive analysis, for the extension of what Polanyi calls 'subsidiary' awareness. On this thesis I am tempted to interpret these comparative data from England and Brazil as being at least indicative that any decision not to provide music education for all children 'cannot be premised on the careless claim that it makes little difference' (Bruner 1972: 67). What is at issue is not whether to educate children but *how*. This is the theme of the final part of this book.

Part III
Musical learning and musical teaching

7 / Teaching for musical knowledge

INTUITION, ANALYSIS AND TEACHING

(1) Every instructor of English knows what quality is. (Any instructor who does not should keep this fact carefully concealed, for this would certainly constitute proof of incompetence.)

(2) Any instructor who thinks quality of writing can and should be defined before teaching it can and should go ahead and define it.

(3) All those who feel that quality of writing does exist but cannot be defined, but that quality should be taught anyway, can benefit by the following method of teaching pure quality in writing without defining it.

(Pirsig 1974/76: 208)

What Robert Pirsig calls a 'method of teaching pure quality' centres on getting students to see for themselves. Instead of writing essays on awkward abstractions such as 'the USA', or the city in which they happen to live, or even just one street, they are asked to think about just one building; 'start with the upper left-hand brick' (p.185). Once again we confront the healthy and natural pull of the intuitive against the analytical. We re-visit the knowledge dialectic from the perspective of teaching and learning. Can we plan a curriculum for what we cannot define? Can we teach what we cannot define? Can we assess what we cannot define? For 'writing' we could very easily substitute 'music'. So let us begin with the musical equivalent of the upper left-hand brick as an entity intuitively grasped and see where it leads in teaching music. In this chapter I shall concentrate on what is sometimes called the general music class, that part of formal music education in schools which – in many countries – is mandatory for all children. The principles brought out here have implications also for college music courses and instrumental teaching, though specialist teaching is given more sustained attention in the following chapter.

I was once asked by Australian colleagues to teach a demonstration lesson in Tasmania, a session lasting for a couple of hours with 25 young people aged around 14 to 15, a local secondary school class. Apparently, each of them was to bring an instrument and the range was wide; from tenor horn to guitar, clarinet, flutes and so on. The assignment was to show how different activities might be integrated within the general music lesson and the given time-span. My first inclination was to play safe, to do something with which I had already had good experiences; after all, a number of teachers would be watching. In the end I decided to risk a project based on an idea I found compelling in a piece of music which had recently re-crossed my path. This 'upper left-hand brick' was a simple set of sound materials, basically a pair of spaced out non-pitched sounds, a sort of rhythmic knock on the door.

Music Example 6
A simple motif

The session began by attending carefully to this scrap of material, noticing how it can be articulated at different speeds, changes which immediately alter the potential expressive charge. Spaced out widely in time, the pair of sounds appear to be fairly 'laid-back'; while crushed up very close together the effect suggests urgency, even alarm. Discharge them at around 160 to the minute, fairly loud, separated by irregular gaps of silence and the expressive effect is, to say the least, of an anxious, worrying character. The insistent, sporadic energy communicates a sense of something undefined but ominous. All this we agreed. The first brick was in place.

The next move was to control and orchestrate this pattern, trying it in ensemble first as a major triad, then as a minor chord, having the instruments enter in layers, building a crescendo, then scaling down in a diminuendo. To achieve this effect the guitars led off first with the louder trumpets brought in last. We now had an outline of a simple piece based on repetition of an 'ominous' pattern, becoming more insistent, then fading away. The brick was not only in place but had multiplied; a small chunk of sound material had been brought under control to serve expressive ends and its repetitions had been organised into a simple but coherent form.

The next step was to organise three groups of around eight people, each group to tackle a specific expressive character task. They had to produce respectively an episode independent of the two-note motif, embodying the feeling of 'mystery', or 'confidence' or 'sadness'; nothing too elaborate and only lasting for up to two minutes or so. No notation was required, unless some graphic aid to the memory was felt to be necessary. After a while we came together and heard the three episodes, checking that they more or less 'worked'. These were then inserted within the scheme of the original overall pattern of the two-note motif.

Music Example 7
A graphic score

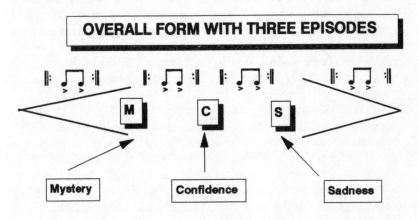

OVERALL FORM WITH THREE EPISODES

Mystery   Confidence   Sadness

The ominous knocking thus interrupted each episode, a linking structural device arousing expectancy as to what might follow. I had to decide when to bring in the whole band; they had to decide when and how to start up their episodes and, of course, what they were to be. We were now working with materials, expression and form.

Something of this same effect is achieved by Wagner in Siegfried's *Funeral March* from *Götterdämmerung* – the piece that came to mind on my way round the world. The life of this operatic hero is reviewed by recalling earlier musical motifs, each one brought up short against the idea of death – the double knock. We listened to a substantial part of this tragic march, I think more attentively than if it had been introduced as 'a part of an opera by Wagner', or I had attempted to recount the far from simple story of The Ring. Without this kind of preparation from the inside of the musical process I would never have risked asking young people of this age to respond to a 'heavyweight' of this kind. Along with other contextual information, knowledge 'that' this work is by Wagner, is – at first – not important. We are really interested in knowledge of music, knowing what we can do with given materials to transform them into expressive entities and build them into structures that hold the attention and lead us further.

We can start intuitively and aesthetically with the materials of any brick we like. But once on the way, engaging with elements of analysis becomes inevitable. The first layer of analysis concerns the impact and management of the materials of a simple motif. The second is to develop strategies for sustaining communicating particular expressive characterisations. The third is to hear the relationships between the motif and the episodes. Building up our own music – or developing an apprehension of someone else's music – soon goes beyond the first impressions of just one brick. We had embarked on an enterprise which made it possible to grasp more of the significance of the great funeral march; an activity in which materials, expression and form are woven together in the warp and weft of intuition and analysis. At the end of the process the students are still left to respond intuitively to music but with the possibility of incremental richness; analytical insights accumulated by listening and doing.

So far, I have tried to expose the main dimensions of musical knowing – materials, expression and form – and shown them at work in research. We now re-visit the first three of these from the practical angle of the general music classroom in school or college. The fourth – the layer of valuing – is rather different. We can to some limited extent anticipate and observe musical valuing but we cannot predict or directly plan for it, except by developing the other layers. Although I shall avoid using abstractions such as 'the teacher' and 'the student', it will become obvious that I am here drawing on experience and observations of teaching, both of others and myself, trying to expose what is important in music education transactions.

ATTENDING TO SOUND MATERIALS

There can be knowledge of the sound materials from which music is fashioned; perceptions of timbre, texture, register, or loudness levels along with the practical skills that give us dependable access to these materials.

Consider the plethora of sounds taken up into music; the vocal range found across the world, instruments that are shaken, plucked, blown, beaten or bowed, sounds that are electronically amplified, modified or generated. Sounds are pressed into musical service that have no single acoustic characteristic making them in some way 'musical'. Many sounds come to us tinged with a strong sense of pitch, others impress us more with their timbre; there are sounds that are marked out by long or short durations and others which have a distinctive quality of loudness or softness. There are only physical dimensions of sound as we perceive it: pitch, timbre, duration, loudness. But we rarely hear them separately; they tend to combine into multiple effects of colour, shape, density, texture. Out of these amalgamations music is made and the possibilities appear to be infinite.

Music can draw upon a vast spectrum of reverberations and there seems no psychological limit to the kind of sound that may be recognised as having musical potential. Any sound can be invested with musical properties, though we ought not to fall into the error of supposing that sound in some way automatically becomes music. Spoken language, for example, involves sound and is not usually construed as music. Indeed, we often ignore the actual sounds of speech in order to concentrate on the linguistic meaning, the message. If we do happen to become more aware of the sonorities, say by repeating a word over and over again, this meaning tends to disappear. The same thing can happen when we listen to people with a regional or foreign accent or friends who have particular vocal mannerisms, such as a slight stammer or a particularly deep vocal register. Under these conditions speech sounds can become so fascinating that we may miss a good deal of what is actually being said and we are thus diverted from the linguistic meaning which has been invested in the sounds. Almost the opposite is true of music. Our attention here is fundamentally towards the behaviour and quality of sound itself. Sound in music and sound in spoken language require different mental attitudes if we are to make sense of them. Our way of listening is different. It is one of the attractions of poetry that literal meaning and sonority run together side by side with equal and complementary importance.

To take another instance of the special way music has with sounds: we frequently distinguish between music and 'noise'. Noise is not unpitched music but simply unwanted sound, sound that distracts us from attending to those particular sounds in which we are interested at the time. One person's music can easily become another's noise, especially music on radios or tape-recorders. The difference between noise and music is mainly a psychological shift, it depends upon a mental attitude. Sound is not heard as a musical phenomenon until it is regarded in a special way; as having intrinsic interest and the possibility of expressive meaning within a context of structural expectations.

In music education during the 1970s – especially in Britain and Canada – 'sound' became a buzz word. Following in the steps of contemporary composers such as John Cage and musician educators such as George Self, Bernard Rands, Brian Dennis, Murray Schafer and John Paynter, there was a proliferation of materials intended for school music teachers bearing such titles as *New Sounds in Class*, *Sound and Silence*, *Exploring Sound*, *Make a New Sound*, *Sounds Fun*, *Sounds Interesting*. The educational principles and activities then being advocated often went beyond exploring sound and it was usually recognised that something important has to happen *with* sound – at least in our imagination – before we are actually engaged with music.

However, the idea was sown that sound might be synonymous with music and some teaching was influenced to the extent that making lists of sounds, inventing new sounds, recording sounds and identifying different categories of sound became supremely important. It was an attempt to begin again, to make a new start, without the clutter of inherited classical traditions which at that time appeared opposed to the growing popular music industry and the musical preferences of many students. 'Ear cleaning' – a term of Murray Schafer's – was encouraged without any limiting preconceptions as to what counts as music, setting aside an inhibiting emphasis on a range of traditional skills and knowledge that were ill-suited to some classrooms and alien to many pupils. In particular, conventional fixed metrical and pitch relationships were often discarded in favour of giving precedence to levels of loudness, texture and tone colour.

This new beginning helped to move some music teachers away from emphasising propositional knowledge to such an extent that by the end of the 1980s teaching facts about music had – in the case of many British schools – become a very small part of music curriculum practice (Swanwick 1989). The focus on sounds was and is necessary and important. Engaging once again in the very first layer of the developmental spiral gives us the feeling of a fresh, uncluttered start. But to evolve as music, sounds have to be managed and shaped. There is much to be said for attending sensitively to the fundamental materials of music; tone-colours, durations of sounds or silences, changes of pitch, levels of loudness, and so on. But there must inevitably be some development of fluency with voices or instruments, awareness of expressive gesture and structural coherence in a stylistic frame.

We can notice how composers and improvisers work from particular and restricted sets of sound materials. It seems essential for us to set boundaries on available sound resources, in order to make music manageable – to get us started. This is why musicians choose to work within the limitations of particular modes and tonal systems, 12-note techniques, pentatonic scales, Indian *raga*, the *maqam* in the Middle East and sets of sound that may be specific to a certain piece; as for instance, when Debussy makes a piano Prelude entirely out of the interval of the third, or when Bartók writes pieces in his *Mikrokosmos* based on 'fifth chords', or 'triplets in 9/8 time', or when jazz musicians improvise on the foundation of a well-known 'standard' tune, or a well-worn blues chord sequence. (See also John Paynter, 1992.)

 Working with limited sets of materials is educationally invaluable in framing and delimiting techniques, in sharpening discriminations, in allowing us to savour the qualities of individual sounds and sound clusters. Students are often involved in compositional studies from starting points in the layer of materials; making a piece of music using perhaps just three notes, or perhaps only a pair of high and low sound clusters, or contrasting loud

Examples of starting from a small point

with soft, or arranging a song with just two chords. Once we attend aesthetically and intuitively to *something* – any 'brick' will do – we can be led on into artistic analysis through multiple possibilities. To bring this out more clearly, here are some instances.

Most of us are familiar with drones in Scottish bagpipe music, though not everyone may be fond of that particular sound. The device of a single held or repeated note (sometimes two or even three) against which is juxtaposed a more mobile set of pitches is by no means limited to Scotland. Bagpipes have existed in most European countries and there is a long tradition in Northumbria, France (Musette), Italy (Cornemuse) and Germany (Dudelsack). And the principle itself, that of a steady pitch allied to a flexible series of pitched sounds has been identified in the ancient world, in all kinds of folk and tribal music, in Arab countries, in Indian *raga*, in popular music and in many compositions by composers in the western world where it is sometimes given the name of 'pedal'. Drones are the earliest and simplest form of harmony and such a widespread use of sound-sets made of drones against rows of notes is understandable. There need be no great technical complexity, yet there are rich possibilities in exploring the tensions and relationships between a fixed pitch and an associated row.

Working in groups or pairs, students can hum or play drones, keeping a single or double sound going by staggered breathing or by agitating strings or pitched bars. At the same time, others can move up and down particular rows of notes which include the drone pitch. The most simple rules are to start and finish on the shared drone note and to maintain the pre-determined order of the note-row; no leaps, at least to begin with. Freedom to discover new possibilities lies in being able to choose speeds, alter the time between and the lengths of notes, adjust levels of loudness, decide whether notes are repeated or not, whether they are played smoothly or detached. Later, these notes can be taken out of the row series and used in any order to invent new melodies, for once the materials – here the pitch relationships – have become familiar to the ear, the sequencing of order becomes a real choice, not accidental or arbitrary. Four or five small groups could take different rows; perhaps a *raga*, a chromatic series, a whole-tone scale (sometimes used by Debussy and Ravel), major or minor scales, modes. There are different expressive possibilities to be sampled from variously constructed rows and we might eventually feel like dropping the drone altogether to focus on the relationships of the pitch sets. An atonal note-row would be a special instance and working with it could be excellent preparation for listening to its use in, say, Schoenberg. An attractive and colourful row is the first five notes of the Phrygian mode – E, F, G, A, B on the keyboard – especially descending, a sound-set of great importance for Miles Davis and his musicians in *Flamenco Sketches*.

Plenty of music comes to mind. The expressively tranquil and relatively uneventful *Pastoral Symphony* in Handel's *Messiah* could easily be adapted for classroom performance and the idea of alternating between a tonic and dominant drone can serve as a basis for group compositions, along with the row (a C major scale) that Handel uses. A striking way to begin a composition is with a drone by itself, especially if it is given rhythmic articulation. Brahms does this with a double drone at the beginning of his *Serenade in D Major* (Opus 11). Again from Brahms – this time from the *German Requiem* and massive in effect – is the single and unchanging drone on 'D' that underpins the chorus, *But the Righteous Souls are in the Hand of God*. The trombones and other bass instruments work in shifts to keep this pedal point going, while the voices and instruments drive the music on and on to the great concluding major chord; such solid certainty to match the meaning of the words. Another instance is found in Tchaikovsky – the *Arabian Dance* from the *Nutcracker Suite*. Here an articulated drone makes a strangely pulsating movement over which delicate woodwind sounds weave smooth lines in thirds. Students can also make tunes in thirds.

But drones and thirds, pedal points and modes, major chords and a *raga* are not concepts, nor should musical pieces be used to illustrate them as though they were. They are particular experiences – bricks in the process of building musical knowledge – knowledge of *this*. From one simple set of sound materials a whole spectrum can open up, with various layers of analysis feeding back into intuitive understanding. A fund of aural and manipulative skill is being acquired that enriches the intuitive apprehension of other music, no matter what style, period or social and ethnic origin. Although the point of departure might be a particular set of sound materials, we come to see that sounds are selected, rejected and brought into coherent relationships with each other. They are also perceived as expressive of particular qualities of feeling; they project character, mood, or atmosphere. Let us then turn to knowledge of music's expressiveness as another educational starting point.

WORKING WITH EXPRESSIVE CHARACTER

There can be knowledge of expressive character; the general atmosphere or mood of a performance, dramatic changes of level, or the specific gesture of a single phrase.

If a person draws, paints or moulds an object in clay, there is likely to be some recognisable image, no matter how stylised or abstract the work may be; some form of imitation, a sense of life beyond the representation; what I have been calling *expressive character*. There is no mystery about this.

Teachers in the arts frequently make fairly direct imitation a focus for classroom or studio work. So in drama, children may role-play, pretending to be someone else or themselves in another setting; or in English lessons they might tell a story from another's point of view, so gaining empathy with that different perspective. In the visual arts they might present a particular object or incident, or – in a more abstract way – render an impression, an overall quality of feeling. In music, imitation extends from the most obvious copying of sounds – bird-song, thunder, clocks, factory machines – to much more subtle characterisations that are 'personal and associative and logical, tinged with affect, tinged with bodily rhythm, tinged with dream', an 'organic experience of vital impulse, balance, conflict, the *ways* of living and dying and feeling' (Langer 1942: 206–7).

We can certainly recognise in music affective qualities and impressions; shrivelling up or opening out, or a sense of increasing stillness or gathering energy without necessarily having visual or other images. Expressive character is not just how we happen to feel but depends on how the *music* sounds. To put it simply, is this a dance or a dirge, a march or a lullaby, does it have a flowing or stamping character? There is no requirement for music to have any external programme, since music is able to abstract feeling qualities and project these in virtual space and time. Music is shot through with suggestive appearances, metaphors of feeling. It can be more or less active, fluid, angular or stationary, more or less dense or heavy, driving forward or holding back; spiky or flowing, smooth or cutting, expansive or contracting.

Musical images are representations, sonorous images of feeling. Without knowing anything of any programmatic background, the first two minutes of *In the South* communicate a sense of great weight and size. But within this general character there are changes and transformations which unceasingly shift the expressive emphasis; just as a good actress playing Lady Macbeth takes us with her through a whole range of moods and reactions – though still contained within the bounds of a credible stage personality, even up to her final disintegration.

Musical expression is worked out through such sound materials as pitch, register, melodic intervals (leaps or steps), phrase shapes, speed, rate of acceleration or retardation, degree of smoothness or detachedness, accentuation, metre and dense or spare textures. Although it is possible to come to know these elements simply as a listener, it is important that students explore and handle these things for themselves, making choices in performance and composition, as well as identifying them in other people's music. With young children especially, it seems best to make, perform and hear pieces that are strongly characterised, where there are clear changes of character, and to look for relationships between their music-making and music-taking. As we have already seen, several encounters may be required to attain the degree of familiarity necessary to identify the particular character of any piece of music. Just as we cannot expect to know a person very well after just one brief meeting, so becoming sensitive to the character and structure of music also requires more than one encounter. Musical knowing is similarly a personal encounter and, as we have seen, it takes time.

There are many ways of sustaining musical encounters and one of these is through physical movement. Dorothy Taylor has produced evidence to suggest that moving to music enhances musical memory – at least the recognition of music on subsequent hearings (Taylor 1989). Might movement encourage more perceptive and detailed listening? For example, we watch a group of children aged 7 and 8 freely moving to part of Birtwhistle's *The Triumph of Time*. They translate the sound blocks, the horns cruising at high altitude and the short dabs of the strings (bars 30–31) into large, flowing gestures punctuated by stabbing movements; moving slowly until a sudden drop of loudness level, at which they cautiously assess the space around them, constricting both forward impulse and lateral motion, some taking on an attitude of questioning by upturned hands and raised shoulders. One girl puts her hand above her eyes as if shading them to peer into the distance.

How will each of them listen to this music in the future and would their perception be different because of this interpretation in movement compared with some other response not so closely analogous with a time-based art, say that of drawing? We suspected this to be true but wanted to investigate the question experimentally.[1] As just one part of this research, two different but similar passages from Birtwhistle's composition were played to a group of children aged 7 to 8 years on different occasions. One extract was interpreted by drawing and the other in movement. In individual structured interviews the passages were played again and we were able to ask them for their account, their analysis, of what they were perceiving. The method was comparatively simple and non-verbal. Six different picture cards of simple stick figures were on the table depicting various expressive attitudes: actively moving forward, more or less still, leaping up, moving forward smoothly, taking on an angular position, heavily drooping. Each child listened and chose as many cards from the piles as seemed to be needed to 'tell the story of the music', laying the pictures out as a form of notation – an analysis of changes over time – along the table in front of them from left to right. It was thus possible to observe not only the number of cards picked up but also the actual order in which they were chosen and at what precise point in listening to the music they were taken.

This procedure was followed for the music of Birtwhistle and also for three other pairs of pieces, each pair being matched by being of similar length and sharing stylistic and expressive features. The movement and drawing responses were alternated throughout the eight sessions, a variation on a quasi-experimental design known as 'the equivalent time-samples design' (Campbell and Stanley 1963: 43) or what Barlow and Hersen call 'the alternating treatment design' (Barlow and Hersen 1984: 253). This is one form of action research, where a teacher working with one group of children has structured her intervention in such a way that she is enabled to make a comparison of responses to music under two different teaching strategies. Teaching in this setting becomes research precisely because the teacher is making a systematic enquiry in addition to being pedagogically active.

The researcher – Mari Shiobara – made her own prior analysis of the music in consultation with other colleagues and felt able to rule out certain card choices as being generally 'inappropriate' at certain times in the score (Shiobara 1993). For instance, when the music seemed to gain forward impulse, to choose an obviously 'passive' card would be counted as an 'inappropriate' description. As it turns out, very few 'inappropriate' cards were chosen – we must never underestimate the sensitivities of children. But many more 'loose' cards were in evidence after they had previously represented (interpreted) the music by drawing than when they had moved to it. This was so for all four pairs of music.

This sequence of teaching and interviewing – first carried out in an English primary school – was later replicated in Tokyo with very similar

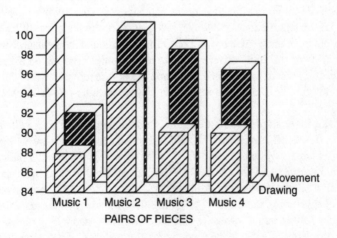

Figure 15 Proportions of 'appropriate' cards: combined results from England and Japan

consequences. Figure 15 shows the combined results from both England and Japan.

Free movement to music seems to focus attention towards the detail and quality of expressive character and appears to create an enduring and lively impression in the mind, not only helping to construe expressiveness but also in following structural change, as one gesture follows or anticipates another. Moving to music appears to be a strongly analogous activity, a form of analysis that stays close to the mobile expressive and structural properties of music: time, pace, weight and forward flow are psychological realities in both movement and music. Movement seems to foster musical knowing, certainly with these young children.

MAKING SENSE OF FORM

There can be knowledge of form, of structural relationships; the way expressive gestures relate to other gestures through the dynamic processes of repetition and contrast, how performances undergo continual metamorphosis and in so doing keep us alert and attentive.

Structure is essentially about internal relationships. In music this involves creating and recognising tendencies that lead us on expectantly or break off to surprise and delight us. In some ways music can be like a joke. So a pattern of repeated rhythms is broken by an abrupt change – a kind of 'punchline' – or the sound of a gong dissolves into a gentle melody. If we are really attending to music we shall find ourselves following streams of ideas which branch out into unpredicted patterns and changes. This involves the awareness of the significance of *change*, recognition of the scale on which events take place, a sense of what is normal in a particular context and what is surprising or strikingly different. These relationships arise within expressive gestures, as when, for instance, the shape of a phrase moves beyond the range of notes first defined and extends itself by wider intervals or in chromatic inflection.

Take for example the first song in the Schumann cycle *Frauenliebe und Leben*. It sets off as a constrained old-fashioned dance, a demure *Sarabande*, over which the widening vocal line mirrors the words speaking of the growth of young love. Already one set of expectations are in tension with another. The first phrase is reshaped sequentially – a way of effecting both repetition and change at the same time. From the end of the seventh bar the vocal line reaches further out, is almost repeated but not quite, and a long phrase gives an impression of subsidence towards the last cadence of the verse: but it is not so final. The move in the bass in the fourteenth bar from an expected B♭ to an F♯ resolving to G, unsettles the course of the music and the close of the

Music Example 8
The beginning of Schumann's *Frauenliebe und Leben* (1840)

verse is necessarily extended. Even then, the final chord is also simultaneously the first chord of the second verse – a piece of structural magic. Here expressive character is heightened, pointed up and extended through structural juxtapositions that convey a sense of disturbance and keep us following expectantly – always of course, depending on the performance.

We can imagine how later on Wagner might have treated the ambiguous cadence, perhaps exploiting the augmented chord without resolution over a longer time period as he does in the *Siegfried Idyll*.

Music Example 9 After Wagner

Or again, we might anticipate how Mahler towards the end of the *Ninth Symphony* would later take this cadential progression and roll it through successive keys, displacing our sense of where the home key really is.

Music Example 10 After Mahler

We here refer to the intellectual satisfaction which the listener derives from following and anticipating the composer's intentions – now to see his expectations fulfilled, and now to find himself agreeably mistaken. It is a matter of course that this intellectual flux and reflux, this perpetual giving and receiving, takes place unconsciously and with the rapidity of lightening flashes – and with perfect justice may be called a pondering of the imagination. Indeed, without mental activity no aesthetic enjoyment is possible.

(Hanslick 1854: 98)

Repetition and similarity with contrast and variety are the main energisers of musical form. All other structural devices are derived in essence from these. To take just a few examples: *ostinato* broken by changes of figure, motifs changed by extension or fragmentation, themes contrasted by middle sections or counter themes, tonic keys set against transposition or modulation, even beats as the basis for syncopations, 'airs' subjected to variation, steady tempo to changes of speed, note-rows to inversion or retrograde motion, acoustic sound to electronic modification. Form is tied up with predicting a future from the evidence of the past, an inevitable part of human nature in life in general and of musical experience in particular (Meyer 1956). Even if music appears to be standing still, timeless in expressive quality and structural evolution – as is sometimes the case with the compositions of Messiaen – this impression still relies upon our image of time. Forward motion is defined by its absence.

Working with structure is a relatively sophisticated task, a development in the minds of children that seems to follow their awareness of materials and expression. How is this phrase, texture or tune different from that? Does anything stay the same? Is any change gradual or sudden? Fruitful classroom activities have included the task of making or identifying surprise in music, finding out how to bring about a sudden contrast or a gradual change, or perhaps how to put two different expressive ideas together in either a conflicting or agreeable relationship.

We might listen to the first of *Five Pieces for Orchestra* by Schoenberg, Opus 16. Intuitively we recognise the dense concentration; things seem to happen quickly in a small soundscape. We hear a warm string sound, slightly urgent – a kind of question? The sounds of woodwind respond, hard and cold – a kind of answer? This happens three times, each time differently and the last answer is positively harsh. There is more movement, pressing in, growing louder. The music turns into a driving march, heavy and powerful, then breaks into fragments which become an echo of the march and it is all over. We could analyse this further by making a version in graphic notation or by listing expressive words in sequence as things change – warm, cold, harsh and so on. Could a series of words or a graphic score be reinterpreted by these students or others as composers, a challenge to work with some structural element in mind?

Whatever the point of departure, music can be *known* and this knowledge is particular and direct; it is knowledge *of* and not merely knowledge *about* music in some general way and this knowledge can be appraised by publicly shared criteria. Critical analysis enhances intuitive response – or it can in sensitive hands. In this way we become connoisseurs, sensitive critics in making and taking music; in the true sense of the term, we are learning to 'read' it. Together, intuition and analysis generate knowledge and the richer the activities are through which such knowledge is acquired, the more likely it is that it will be meaningful, personally significant.

INTEGRATING MUSICAL ACTIVITIES

The idea that composing, performing and audience-listening are activities that reinforce one another has strong support in the literature on music education and can be observed as an organising principle in much effective teaching (Leonhard and House 1959, Swanwick 1979, Plummeridge 1991, Regelski 1983). There is an assumption that these activities are somehow interdependent, a view we find, for example, in Janet Mills.

> In an integrated and coherent music education in which children compose, perform and listen, the boundaries between musical processes disappear. When children compose, for instance, they cannot help but learn as performers and listeners.
>
> (Mills 1991: 87)

There appears to be little research to support this intuition or indeed to substantiate the reverse position, which is that listening to music enhances children's development as composers – even though it does seem likely. One reason for the lack of evidence is the difficulty of assessing music-making in order to observe the effect of one activity on another. But since we can feel reasonably confident about the validity and reliability of criteria derived from the musical development spiral, it becomes possible to test the hypothesis in at least one direction: that audience-listening may have a positive effect on the way students compose.

To investigate this hypothesis, Michael Stavrides extended his research with children in Cyprus schools. Four age groups were identified in four corresponding schools; 4/5, 8/9, 11/12, 14/15. In each of these four schools matched experimental and control groups of ten children were selected. The four teachers involved each followed a similar plan of action. The focus of the project was 'contrasts' and recordings of pieces embodying clear contrasts by Grieg and Mussorgsky were available only to the children in the experimental groups, with whom the teachers organised listening sessions. Then followed two opportunities to compose and record compositions and to use any form of notation that seemed appropriate. All students in both groups had two opportunities to compose a piece based on the idea of 'contrasts' and both groups worked with the same teacher.

Nine experienced independent observers – music teachers – were asked to listen to a random sample of these compositions, selected only on the basis of having 16 representative compositions from each age group, eight from each of the control and experimental classes. They assessed these compositions using the criterion statements described earlier and Figure 16 shows the resulting distribution of levels, a pattern which is statistically significant.[2]

From this we can see that there is a marked difference between the

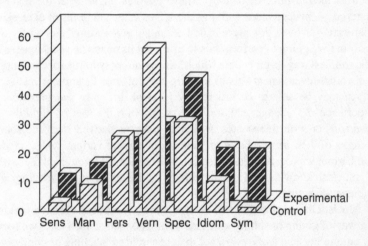

Figure 16   Compositions from Cyprus schools

compositions of experimental and control groups. The children who had taken part in an activity which at least had the possibility of them integrating audience-listening and their own composing appear to be attracting assessments at higher levels. We are still working to see if the reverse is also a sustainable hypothesis; if and how practical activities might positively influence the perception of music in the audience-listener mode. It does appear though that there may be a demonstrable and predictable interdependence between composing and audience-listening and this is not really so surprising. Ideas from the music of other people are assimilated into the working processes of all composers, with positive outcomes. Music teaching and learning can be structured in ways that enhance this interaction between assimilation and accommodation, between intuition and analysis.

The educational process advocated here is simple. We start not from 'concepts' but from music and we end with it; beginning with intuitive response to music and then analysing *by ear* some perceived feature of materials, character or form. This reality forms the basis of practical classroom activities. The essential component is that teachers behave musically – both as critics and models.

Of course there are other ways of working, but given a choice, my preferred procedure is to work from musical *features* intuitively drawn from music 'out there' and not initially from analytical abstractions, 'concepts' such as metre, mode or melody. These features might be at the level of materials – 'make a piece with just these five notes'; in terms of expressive character – 'why is this piece called *Shadows in the Rain*?' ; or as form – 'how are we going to perform this to bring out its contrasts and surprises?'. The simplest way – a procedure which has obvious possibilities of curriculum sequential development – is to identify 'sets of sound', units of materials which may be able to be ordered by level of difficulty and prerequisite experience. So younger children may work with the sets of high/low or loud/soft, or with three notes or rhythm patterns derived from the sound patterns of their names. Later on they might explore various scales, modes and harmonic progressions. These can be experienced through all the layers of musical knowing and in the related activities of music-making and audience-listening.

Much of this exploration will involve student choice and decision-making – a way of giving breathing space for intuition – and at each level we focus on unique musical *features*, rather than generalised labelling or conceptual classification. Even so, by the end of schooling, students should have a pretty good knowledge map of what kinds of music are around and where they can be found. They will be able to do this because intuitive understanding has been nurtured by discriminating analysis and relevant contextual information centred on real musical experiences as composers, performers and audience-listeners. A map is no substitute for being there but it is helpful to possess one if we really intend to travel.

Analysis need not always be through notations or in words but is energised whenever we thoughtfully make decisions in rehearsal, in discussion or when moving to music. Effective music teachers seem to understand this. I am not then suggesting anything new but merely trying to say why they are effective; they appreciate that music is an intrinsic, primary form of analysis of human experience, a way of interpreting the world; they know that sensitive analysis feeds intuitive understanding; they know what *quality* is, even if they find it difficult to define.

8 Instrumental teaching as music teaching

LEARNING TO LEARN

On the surface, and compared with general music teaching, instrumental instruction appears to be relatively uncomplicated by considerations of knowledge and value. I play an instrument; therefore I can show you or anyone else how to play it. But life is not quite so simple, and there is a great deal involved in any educational transaction. In many ways instrumental teaching seems a very haphazard affair with idiosyncratic extremes, depending on the individual teacher who can be somewhat isolated in the confines of the music room or studio. We may think that the instrumental student simply wants to learn to play an instrument, but what does that mean? There are ways of teaching the trombone or the bass guitar that open up the way into musical playing and musical understanding more effectively than others, that are either a part of an initiation process into musical discourse or are not.

Getting people to play any instrument without musical understanding – not really 'knowing music' – is an offence against human-kind. It denies both feeling and cognition and under such conditions the world becomes meaningless. Discourse is stripped of significance, shorn of quality; intuitive understanding is driven out and the knife of technical analysis cuts away to the bare bone. Some of the most disturbing teaching I have witnessed has been in the instrumental studio, where – in a one-to-one relationship giving the teacher considerable power – a student can be confronted simultaneously by a complex page of notation, a bow in one hand and a violin in the other, along with exhortations to play in time, in tune, with a good tone. On the contrary, some of the very best teaching has been by instrumentalists. For example, take this case study, a description by Christine Jarvis of children at work as part of the Tower Hamlets project in London primary schools.

> The violins were tuned by the teacher while each child bowed the open-strings. This prepares children for the time when they are able to tune their own instruments, familiarising them with both the sound and

the process, though in most group lessons violins are pre-tuned to save time. The teacher then distributed 'practise sheets' with four tunes written out in note names or Sol-fa.

The lesson proceeded with a revision of the bow-hold, and attention to general posture, followed by a performance of *Hoe Down*, which was played once more. *Cowboy Chorus* was then performed several times, the children walking round in a circle as they played, three or four being invited to improvise answering phrases between each performance of the tune. The leader then introduced a sight-reading game, 'spin-a-tune', and a few minutes were spent reading through a piece, examining the rhythm and naming the notes before playing it.

The lesson continued with work on the D-major scale, first singing it to Sol-fa, then playing it using rhythms chosen by the children based on short sentences including colour, animal, action, place. Some amusing sentences were produced, making quite long rhythms. Posture and bow-hold were checked again, and the lesson concluded with *Ringing Bell* played with varied bowings, including tremolo and spiccato.

The pace was fast, with active involvement and lively participation of the children throughout. Teaching was very child-centred and made technical work fun by using a variety of games. The teacher always finds things to which they can relate.

Group Lessons: The 3rd-year and 4th-year (92 children in all) are usually divided into two groups for simultaneous lessons in the two school halls. On this occasion, with a Christmas concert looming, the morning began by rehearsing Christmas songs. The teaching team was present, as were all the class teachers involved. Eight songs were practised, some in a less traditional version, the words of one or two being adapted. For example in *The 12 Days of Christmas*, *Five Gold Rings* became *Five Ripe Mangoes*, and so on. Other songs included two rounds and three other seasonal songs, two of which were sung as a duet. Attention was directed to intonation, and there was some rhythmic practise. The project teacher was helping to prepare all the classes in the school for the Christmas concert and was observed in a lively session with infants and nursery children in the afternoon, all class teachers being present.

Following the morning singing session, they divided into two string groups. The smaller group (17 violins and three 'cellos) were given a lesson centred on bowing technique in two pieces. Some time was spent practising slurred bowing in preparation for one of these pieces. Notation was also revised and fingering sung before playing pieces through. This lesson was more technical than the average large group session.

Meanwhile, the noticeably less advanced large group (52 children), rehearsed some items for the school Christmas concert. These included *Hoe Down* and open-string versions of both *Jingle Bells* and *Silent Night* with the melody played on the piano. A Bengali teacher learns the violin with the group, and one or two other class teachers were present, including the deputy head. This group do not have back-up lessons. The emphasis in this lesson was essentially on the enjoyment of the musical experience.

(Swanwick and Jarvis 1990: 27–8)

The teaching and learning described in this passage were fairly typical of sessions in the *Tower Hamlets String Teaching Project*, now unfortunately closed down through a policy of removing education budgets from town halls and putting money directly into schools. This remarkable scheme achieved an international reputation. The essence of the project was to bring a team of musician-teachers into regular contact with unselected classes of children in primary schools – mainly in the East End of London – and to make music a constant feature in the life of the school. The main lessons with whole classes of around 25 unselected children were backed up by work in smaller groups where there was a more technical focus. The complexities of playing a stringed instrument were not tackled by narrowing down attention to one way of approaching music or by confining activities to one style of practising or to hacking through a tutor book page by page. Musical learning in these schools took place through multi-faceted engagement: singing, playing, moving, listening to others, performing in different size groups, integrating the various activities we associate with music. Those teachers responsible for bringing this about saw their job as teaching music through an instrument, not just teaching the instrument. They understood that musical knowledge has several strands, different levels of analysis; and they left space for intuitive engagement – where all knowledge begins and ends.

Even at the level of 'knowing how' – the psycho-motor technical management of an instrument – there are insights to be won into how we actually learn complex skills and sensitivities, gaining control over sound materials. The simple view of what happens would be to assume that a skilled action – say playing *Hoe Down* on a violin – is the result of tying together into one bundle a number of smaller technical bits into a larger whole, rather like making a broom or a peg rug. But do we really build up a technique from individual bristles, from atoms of muscular behaviour? The element of truth in this is rather small and needs a massive correction. Above all the performance of a skill requires a *plan*, a blueprint, a *schema*, an action pattern.

When I run towards a moving tennis ball – hoping to hit it back over the net – I am not just stringing together a number of totally separate physical movements of legs, arms, hand and so on. I am coordinating hand, eye and body into a unique variation on a known theme, called 'getting the ball back'. When I play a piece on the piano or trombone I am not only drawing on specific bits of knowledge but will be executing a plan, a blueprint, managing the piece in accordance with a set of requirements 'in my head', which unfolds and to some extent changes as we go along. Once I lose the thread of the plan – perhaps by getting behind in my musical thinking – or perhaps too far in front of the unfolding moment – then things tend to fall apart.

Building up a representation or *schema* seems to be facilitated by varied practice. For instance, I might stand in front of a dart-board or archery target practising hitting the bull's-eye. But if I always stand in exactly the same practice position with the same weight of arrow or dart and then eventually test myself with a fixed number of tries I am likely to be less successful than if I had the same number of practice shots from different distances, perhaps with differing weights of projectile. I am forming a *plan*, an image of how to throw at a dart-board or shoot at a target, not acquiring a set of automated muscular tricks from a fixed position. In any case, it is impossible to perform any action twice in exactly the same way. Seeing the target and feeling the action from differing perspectives helps me to get the plan in better shape; there seems to be more of mind at work. Variable practice has been shown to be important in *schema* formation (Schmidt 1975). When teaching music, educators have always suspected this to be true and good instrumental teachers have found ways of getting their students to play the same material – perhaps scales or pieces – slowly, quickly, detached, *legato*, in dotted rhythms, with accents falling in different places, using alternative fingerings or hand positions and so on. This variety and depth of approach was characteristic of the Tower Hamlets project, where children clapped, moved, played, sang and listened to music.

We are also helped to form plans by the use of metaphors, mental images, mind pictures of the action. For example, I want to take hold of a 'cello bow in a way that conforms both to the shape of my hand and the stick and allows me maximum flexibility and control in action. One fairly common approach seems to be to try to sort out the position of each finger in turn, perhaps having a teacher move my hand about or place appropriate fingers at the right angles and in the right places. But that would be the teacher's plan, not *mine* and things are likely to go wrong when I am left on my own. Alternatively, I could put my hand in a 'pretend' bucket of water and shake off the drops – now the hand and arm are free and loose. Then – following an idea of Phyllis Young – I might imagine that I take up a fairly soft strawberry between thumb and second finger, applying this 'plan' to the bow itself (Young 1978). Through a series of metaphors and drawing on an existing repertoire of movements, I come to be in control of my own bow-hold and will have begun to generate a *schema* or plan of my own – a mental picture which can be refined and further developed. In developing images of action a student is learning how to manage music, becoming autonomous, learning how to learn. How different all this is from a teacher pushing my fingers around – something that is done to me rather than anything that *I* am doing. Unfortunately it seems that much instrumental teaching tends not to be informed by this realisation.

Fiona Pacey studied the effect of introducing varied practice over an eight-week period, during which a number of young string players between the ages of 8 and 12 were asked to work with their teachers to test out the strength of the hypothesis (Pacey 1993). In one of a number of experimental projects the particular set of sound materials to be brought further under control concerned loudness levels: the ability to play a passage quietly or loudly, a skill in string playing which depends crucially on the movement and weight of the right arm, the speed and amount of bow and, of course, the monitoring ear. After some weeks of 'normal' teaching, the teachers moved to a more intensive variable practice schedule, where, during three sessions, they had the students use a great variety of bowing actions using several parts of the bow. In organising practice towards this end the teachers did not limit themselves to practising only the required simple *forte* and *piano* difference. That would be rather like always standing at the same position during target practice. Before and after this intervention, each pupil was recorded on tape playing the tune *Lightly Row*, a relatively easy piece marked with required changes of loudness level indicated by *f* and *p*, in basic notation which they all understood.

Music Example 11 Lightly Row

Altogether there were 47 instrumentalists playing violin, viola or 'cello and these were taught by nine different teachers in small groups. The project was organised within an overall time schedule that randomised the placing of the intervention of variable practice. So group 'A' began to work in this way after the third observation (recording), group 'B' after the second and group 'C' after the fourth observation. Thus, although the whole project spanned eight weekly sessions, students from any single group were recorded in only six performances, the 'observations' – 'O'. For example, the schedule for Group 'A' was as follows.

$$O^1 \qquad O^2 \qquad O^3 \qquad \text{INTERVENTION} \qquad O^4 \qquad O^5 \qquad O^6$$

The research design is a time series based on product analysis – judges listening to the playing of the students. Repeated observations over a time series are a more ecologically sensitive way of gathering data than 'one-shot' testing. The situation is quite complex though and, as we might predict, there is a good deal of variance between individual pupils, those playing different instruments and groups with particular teachers. Seven independent observers – all teachers and members of performing groups – were asked to assess on a low to high continuum the level of success in playing *forte* and *piano*. Six performances of every student were presented to them on tape-recordings – in random order of course – with no prior knowledge of which student was which. The assessments of these 'judges' were then averaged to help us look for estimated change over time.

As expected, there is a general upward trend over the six occasions of measurement. We always tend to optimistically assume that playing improves over time and with teaching. Taking all three groups together there was a suggestion that the slope of the upward trend increased slightly after the intervention point, though because of the relatively small numbers involved and the complications of pupil, teacher and instrumental variables this cannot be confirmed to a level of statistical significance.

It is worth looking more carefully at one of the larger groups – the 17 pupils in group 'A'. With this group the introduction of varied practice began at the end of the third session, just following the third observation (recording). The next session included quite a range of varied practice with different bow lengths and this was continued into the fifth session, at the end of which the fourth observation took place. Figure 17 shows the pattern of change for students in this group.

Inspection of these data suggests a fairly sharp increase in the upward slope after the intervention with the varied practice programme. Looking a little closer at the data, we can also see a difference between those students whose earlier performances of *Lightly Row* were rated by the expert judges to be on the low side in terms of loudness control and those whose performances from the start were already perceived to demonstrate control of the bow

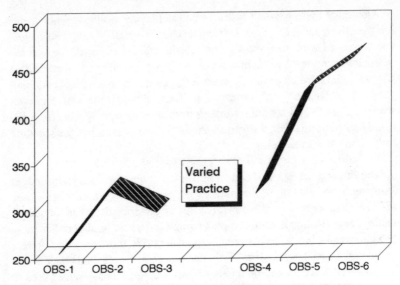

Figure 17   Control of loudness on string instruments: Group A – 17 players

to produce different loudness levels. Figure 18 shows this pattern. It is interesting if not surprising to notice that those students given initial high ratings by the teacher-judges appear to change little over time. There is obviously a limit to the amount of improvement to be expected beyond what is already a good performance. After a time any task gets to be insignificant in its level of challenge. However, the ten students with first-time lower ratings produce a steep climb in managing changes of loudness level following the intervention as can be seen in Figure 18, overleaf.

Variable practice in this case really did seem to pay off, though mostly for those students who initially were not able to manage control of loud and soft playing so very well, while the more advanced students appeared to improve hardly at all. This is not so surprising; we are hardly likely to become more fluent in a skill which is already well under control. Such results are encouraging, an analysis of what we already intuitively suspect to be true, carried out as far as possible under research conditions. Approaching technical control from several different angles facilitates learning. It makes sense. If I can play a piece in only one way – perhaps at one speed with one level of articulation – then things are likely to go adrift fairly easily and the whole thing can break down when something untoward happens. But if I have practised altering the expressive character by adjusting speed, accentuation and relative loudness levels, then not only is my technique likely to be

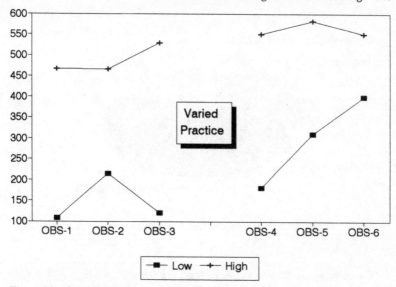

Figure 18 Control of loudness on string instruments: high and low starts

improved but the chances of an interesting performance are raised. Musical decisions are being taken.

Giving time to experiment with music in various ways does two things. Firstly it lets in the prospect of intuitive insights, unconsciously coming to new ways of approaching the performance; secondly, it supplies alternative slices of analysis, bringing to consciousness a broader repertoire of expressive possibilities. Often it seems that instrumental students are confronted with one technical hurdle after another with little musical gratification on the way, no sense of accomplishment and hardly any chance to make performance judgements for themselves. Playing becomes mindless and routine, and musical knowledge is neither gained nor projected to an audience. Two educational settings are especially likely to produce this unhappy state of affairs; one is the individual lesson and the other the very large group with one instructor. In the first there is a tendency to be pushed mainly into technical mastery to the exclusion of musical judgements; in the second it is all too easy to become another cog in a machine.

An account by Kevin Thompson of his study of instrumental teachers at work suggests that attention tends to be focused on aural, manipulative and notational skills and on teaching technical terminology. Figure 19 shows the proportion of time spent by four fairly typical teachers in various ways during weekly lessons over one month. These students were aged between 9 and 12 years and they were playing wind, brass and string instruments.

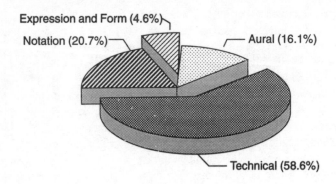

Figure 19   Use of time in instrumental lessons: four teachers observed four times

The emphasis within instrumental teaching that we see here is pretty clear. Technical work and technical talk seems to be the order of the day and there may be good reasons for this. Sessions are often short and teachers want to be sure that students are getting into 'good habits'. Without technique nothing is possible. Since technique itself appears to be enhanced by varied practice, we need to be sure that we are not just grinding away within a narrow set of routines. Playing passages in one way may not be the best way to meet even the limited aim of acquiring a manipulative skill. In general, it would be better to have students play more pieces in different ways and at lower levels of manipulative difficulty, than always to press on relentlessly with the next exacting assignment, a strategy which leaves no time for intuition or analysis and keeps the discourse in the studio fixed on the level of mastery of materials.

GROUP INTERACTION

One way of broadening the instrumental teaching agenda is through work in groups. I ought to make it clear that I am not advocating group teaching exclusively, nor am I denigrating the private teacher. I simply want to draw attention to some of the potential benefits of group teaching as just one valuable strategy in instrumental instruction. To begin with, music-making in groups has infinite possibilities for broadening the range of experience, including critical assessment of the playing of others and a sense of perform- ance. Music is not only performed in a social context but is learned and understood in such a context. Music and music learning involves building up plans, images, *schemata*, through ways of thinking, practising, playing and responding; learning by imitation of and comparison with other people. We are strongly motivated by observing others and we strive to emulate our peers, often with a more direct effect than being instructed by those persons designated as 'teachers'. Imitation and emulation are particularly strong between people of similar ages and social groups. The basic requirements for anyone playing an instrument are careful listening and perceptive watching. A group with a good teacher is an ideal circumstance for the development of these attitudes. We might think of 'master-classes' where everyone present can learn something. Giving attention to someone else's sound, posture, style of playing and technical achievement, is all part of group motivation; so is the stimulation of other people's triumphs and the consolation of recognising their difficulties. There is here scope for intuitive knowledge, learning by osmosis.

Group teaching is not at all the same as teaching individuals who happen to be scheduled in a group, giving attention to each of them, say, on the basis of ten minutes each over half an hour. Working with a group is a totally different form of educational endeavour. To start with, the teacher has to be especially alert. There can be no casual drifting into lessons without previous preparation. There can be no listening with half an ear whilst looking out of the window, consulting the diary of engagements or attending to the length of one's fingernails. There are constant questions to be addressed. What is the next stage of development and where do we go from here? How do we involve all students at all times?

Involvement does not mean only the physical activity of playing the instrument. In a group, an important activity will be listening and diagnosing, discussing and trying-out. One of the most striking things about good group teaching is this degree and range of participation of all group members. Every teacher will remember the kind of experience where we feel, 'If only so-and-so were able to hear this', or 'how much time might be saved if I could get all these people together'. Group-teaching does not exclude individual help and is certainly not 'anti-technique'. Kevin Thompson observed his four teacher-colleagues at work with individual students and also with groups of up to eight people. By systematically observing an individual in each group who was 'matched' as closely as possible with a student having individual lessons, Thompson found that:

> ... individual and group-taught students received more or less the same spread of time to the various aspects of learning in music, with the exception of notational skills. In spite of group-taught students having received less time in this category, their level of achievement in fluency of notation was disproportionately high. Perhaps teachers made fewer repetitive statements in group settings and saved instructional time. This,

coupled with the possibility of learning from others, may account for the alacrity with which the group-taught students acquired notational skills.

(Thompson 1984: 168–9)

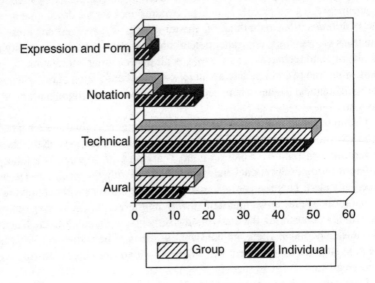

Figure 20   Group and individual teaching: focus of attention

No more time was spent 'off task' or setting up equipment in group settings than in individual lessons and Thompson observed that, while students in groups seemed to be acquiring a wider range of skills in more varied musical and social conditions, the teachers behaved very differently when working with groups, with positive changes in levels of preparedness, interaction and personal dynamism. From interviews he conducted with 14 experienced group instrumental teachers, he concluded that they saw instrumental groups as educationally valuable rather than as an economical necessity and that working with groups was the preferred mode of teaching, though they recognised the necessity at times for individual instruction.

Resistance to instrumental group-teaching most often comes from those who have come through music schools and *conservatoires* where the one-to-one ratio is jealously preserved and no other alternative seems feasible. Yet we recognise that people can learn a great deal by sitting next to other players in a brass band, guitar class, a rock group, or as a member of a chorus. There is an obvious example here in the school and college bands of North America. In these essentially large-scale teaching groups of mixed instruments, people learn much of their playing technique and stylistic understanding from within the group itself. I would not advocate this necessarily as the best way of organising instrumental learning but refer to it merely in order to point out that the one-to-one way of working is an extreme at the opposite end of a spectrum.

How much time in lessons is spent on common problems? Is there anything to be learned from regular participation in a small ensemble? Are there not dull lessons when both teacher and pupil feel lethargic, tired, uninspired and might not a group even out the ups and downs of personal temperament and present a constantly stimulating challenge to teachers who are really interested in teaching?

It is unwise to teach individuals on a kind of deficit model; they bring along their mistakes to the lesson and we try to sort them out. This is neither possible nor desirable in a group setting. Good group teachers know how to structure sessions to avoid mistakes and misunderstanding from the outset. A group should be large enough to be a potential music-making ensemble but small enough for any individual to play a distinctive part. A number somewhere between six and 15 tends be seen as optimum by those who work with groups. The major requirement is that the teacher has to prepare beforehand; the major benefit is that – under the cover of a group environment – the pupil can be learning on the intuitive side as well as taking part in a range of analytical work that will lead towards student autonomy, freedom from the teacher.

LITERACY OR FLUENCY?

Staff notation seems to have a curious effect on musical behaviour and it certainly has a strong influence on instrumental teaching and playing. The greatest virtue of written signs is their potential for communicating certain details of performance that would easily be lost in aural transmission, just forgotten. Imagine what would happen if the production and preservation of any large-scale classical symphonies had been entirely dependent on the collective memories of composers and performing groups. It is inconceivable that many if any of these works could have been composed at all without the visual maps and designs that constitute the making of a score. But imagine also what happens if these scores are converted either by machine or by mechanical playing into sound, as for example, in the distinctive regularity of fair-ground organs. Without aural performance traditions, most expressive and structural shaping is missing. Worse, imagine the consequences of insisting on notating jazz, rock, a *raga* improvisation or almost any folk music *before* performance. Such a needless exercise would impede fluency and stifle creative thought. Yet in instrumental teaching within the western classical tradition, notational 'literacy' is thought to be essential and thus notation is often central to instruction and is frequently the starting point.

This apparent tension between improvisation and notation has bothered educators for some time. Consider Kodály: 'Millions are condemned to musical illiteracy, falling prey to the poorest of music' (Kodály 1974: 119–204). He thought that every child by the year 2000 should be able to read music and every detail of his *Choral Method* leads towards this goal. On the other hand, for Dalcroze, music reading came second to feeling music in movement. Orff considered notation to be important but his emphasis is on making music rather than reading it. Although Kodály advocated improvisation we hear very little about it in the *Choral Method*. For Dalcroze, improvisation had a very important function, to awaken the 'motor tactile consciousness'. For Orff the central principle of his *Schulwerk* was not the performance of written-out music with ready-made accompaniments but, as he said a 'continuous inventing', though imitation is the 'beginning of improvisation'. Orff is looking for a 'spontaneous art of discovery with a hundred ways and a thousand possible structures' (Thomas in Keetman 1974: 13).

Music educators and other musicians do seem to agree that one goal of music education should be to help people to develop what is sometimes called the 'inner ear', a 'dynamic library' of musical possibilities which we draw on in performance. Jazz musicians certainly have strong views on improvisation. I made notes at a conference I was chairing in London, where jazz players extolled the virtues and essential nature of improvisation. In brief summary, the collective wisdom of this group appeared to be as follows:

* everyone can improvise from the first day of playing;
* the basic principle is to have something fixed and something free, the fixed including scale, riff, chord, chord sequence and – crucially – beat;
* it is possible to make great music at any technical level;
* use systems but beware of fixed, rigid teaching strategies;
* imitation is necessary for invention and copying by ear is a creative effort;
* improvisation is characterised by problem-solving and a high level of personal interaction;
* there is no consensus as to how people can be helped to practise improvisation – commitment leads to self-tuition and the motivation is 'delight';
* improvisation is self-transcending not self-indulgent and the product

matters, we make contact with something beyond our own experience, it makes demands upon the way we listen;
* the secret of playing jazz is the aural building of a 'dynamic library'.

There is no mention of notation here, yet once again we can identify the intuition/analysis dialectic. Improvising is the development and demonstration of a retrieval system and intuition is its essential process. The spotlight of the mind that searches what we already know for what is relevant *at this time* is guided, not by conscious thought, but by intuitive scanning. But as we know, intuitive knowledge can only grow if it is complemented by analytical mapping; and this includes identifying the 'something fixed', both channelling and extending the way we listen. 'Copying', imitating, are themselves acts of analysis where we sift out certain elements for attention – those things we want to emulate. Varied practice is also analytical, a way of consciously extending the dynamic library, cataloguing, classifying, building up a *schema*, an action pattern.

The 'inner ear' is essentially the forming of musical images and this faculty is developed through the interaction of intuitive musical expression and analytical sifting. All musical performance is inevitably 'playing by ear' and an astute analysis of this curious term by Philip Priest brings out clearly the diverse educational activities that fall under the common terminology. His definition of 'playing by ear' is comprehensive: 'all playing that takes place without notation being used at the time' (Priest 1989). The categories below point to some of the various possibilities:

* memorised signs, where the player's memory of the notation from which the music has been learned is used as a visual aid;
* imagined signs, where the player constructs such signs for the first time as an aid to finding pitch notes;
* imitation of a model (seen and heard), where both the physical actions and sounds they produce are observed and copied;
* imitation of a model (heard only), the copying of a pattern or tune based on what is heard – whether live or recorded;
* imitation of imagined sound, where the player attempts to reproduce remembered tunes or patterns;
* improvised variation, altering the original music (read or remembered) by elaboration but keeping to the structure;
* invention within a framework, playing from a sketch (chord symbols or figured bass) in the prevailing rhythm and style;
* invention with no framework, sometimes called extemporisation, the player being free to choose every aspect of the music;

* experimental invention, discovering sounds and nuances new to the
player and perhaps to music.

(Priest 1989: 174)

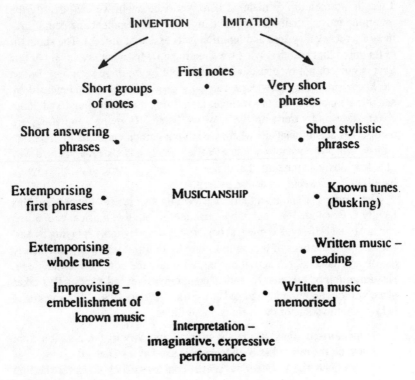

Figure 21 A pedagogical model of instrumental learning
Source: Priest (1989)

Priest derives a pedagogical model from this – seen in Figure 21 – an
analysis which greatly assists us to envisage a range and depth of teaching
possibilities.

Musical activities often involve more than one of the processes shown in
Figure 21 at the same time and any player may be more or less conscious of
them – more or less intuitive or analytical. Analysis takes place whenever
we stop to think, sort out a fingering or choose to separate out a strand or
section for practise. Using notation of any kind is always a form of analysis;
certain elements of music are abstracted, taken out of the dynamic library for
inspection and given special attention, perhaps pitch or rhythm relationships

or chord sequences. As Priest says, it has been assumed amongst music educators that skill with musical notation with its implicit underlying analysis is essential for an 'understanding' of music. The concept of 'musicianship' in music curricula is often closely tied in with notational skills and certain limited kinds of aural tests. Yet the value of notation as a remembering and transmitting device is not always needed and is now more than ever under question, thanks to micro-technology and especially sophisticated recording techniques. In much music-making it is no longer essential. As an analytical performance and compositional tool it can have value but only if the analysis is in the first place and ultimately aural. Priest again:

> Naming notes and recognising signs are *ancillary* skills for a player, not essential to performance nor to understanding if by understanding we mean *thinking in sounds* and *being able to appreciate and convey artistic expression through music*.
>
> (Priest 1989: 175, italics in original)

The alternative may be that students just 'bark at print' – a phrase used to refer to reading out aloud without any real sense of meaning. Listening to some students practising the piano is rather like having me read Mandarin from a phonetic transcription. I would have no idea what it means and it must sound dreadful. There must be better ways.

THE FOURTH FINGER ON THE A STRING

Daniel is seven. He now has a half-size 'cello which not only looks wonderful but can – in the right hands – sound well too. Why a 'cello? Someone came to his school and played one. Thereafter he wanted to play 'a big instrument like the 'cello'. When taken to the first half of a concert which included Strauss's *First Horn Concerto* and seated on the front row, he resolutely ignored the horn soloist in front of his nose and scrutinised the 'celli. Why this should be is hard to know. Visual and aural images of instrumentalists playing seem to linger in the memory and perhaps there are ranges of instrumental sonority that seek out particular people as if to say 'Hi! you're on my wavelength, my sound spectrum coincides with your way of taking the world'. Sound materials are wonderfully compelling, even before the music starts. They are the beginning and the end of musical experience.

We have a recommended tutor book but, when getting him started at home, I am puzzled by the titles of the pages: 'fourth finger on the A string', and by the captions within pages: 'the bow-hold', 'ledger lines', 'basic knowledge' (which turns out to be about the notation of the bass clef), 'the minim', 'the semibreve rest'. This particular slice of musical analysis fails to captivate Daniel and it worries me.

I do not even play the 'cello, beyond the most elementary level, but I have worked intensively with string players and I think I know what matters. They care about the sound they make, they know that string sonorities can be powerfully evocative and that the instruments have all sorts of potential (how near the bow is to the bridge or fingerboard, which part of the bow is appropriate, off or on the string) and they like their playing to be coherent, structured. Just wandering through a piece is no way to play it.

So we begin. 'Pluck each string in turn four times – yes anchor your right thumb lightly against the side of the finger-board'. Now let's get the bow to work. 'Try pulling it across the 'C' string and then pushing it back again' (first getting the fresh strawberry hold) and 'feel the sound in your chest'. 'Now the next string.' I am soon becoming a pianist expert in vernacular patterns based on the open strings of the 'cello, and these figures organise our music-making. They include horn calls, dramatic *tremolo*, flowing divisions of the beat that lead us on to the next change of string and Latin American rhythm patterns (especially the *habanera* or *tango*) that seem to fall under the bow so effectively. We are making music and it is the first lesson. In time we shall explore other sets of sound, including the up and down patterns of left-hand fingers on the A string – especially the difference between C and C♯ which so strongly affects expressive character.

This personal account – a small case-study description, a thumb-nail sketch of an encounter with music – serves only to press the point that instrumental teaching must be *musical* teaching, not merely technical instruction on the instrument. There is no point in teaching music at all unless we believe that it is a form of human discourse and that the beginning instrumental player is being initiated from 'day one' into this discourse and not into 'the semibreve rest'. Analysis on only a narrow technical level and without intuitive response leads nowhere. Perhaps this is why so many instrumental students give up. In *Music, Mind and Education* I characterised the apparent analysis/intuitive rift as a tension between instruction and encounter.

...this tension between instruction and encounter is both inevitable and fertile. These apparently contradictory aspects of human learning are the positive and negative poles between which the electricity of educational transactions flow. Encounter and instruction correspond with the left and right of the musical spiral, with the natural ebb and flow of musical experience. To some extent, it is possible to proceed by instruction in the acquisition of manipulative skills, vernacular conventions, idiomatic tra-

ditions, systematic procedures. Here, learning can be more easily structured and sequenced. But it is encounter that characterises the left hand
side: sensory impression, personal expression, structural speculation and
symbolic veneration. Here, the student needs to be left alone with possibilities, many of which will exist thanks to some instructional framing.
Theories and practice of music education that fail to acknowledge a
dynamic relationship between left and right, leave us trying to clap with
one hand.

(Swanwick 1988: 135)

Rule number one: no lesson is in order without music and music means
delight and control of materials, heightened awareness of expression and
whenever possible the delight of good form. A session without music is time
wasted and the wrong message is taken away – that it is sometimes in order
to play unmusically. It is *never* in order.

Rule number two: always go for intuitive fluency before analytical literacy. In the early days at least, music should be articulated freely before
sorting out notation. We do not need the limited analysis of a printed copy
in front of our faces *every* time we play. Aural awareness precedes and is the
foundation, the real 'rudiments of music'; it is also the end-game of musical
knowledge.

Rule number three: by all means push but also pull. Students can be drawn
into what they sense to be worthwhile. How well do we and other people play
for and with the student? Is music an invitation? Students need to feel that
what they do contributes to sustaining human mind, we all do.

Instruction without encounter, analysis without intuition, artistic craft
without aesthetic pleasure; these are recipes for educational disaster. Meaningless action is worse than no activity at all and leads to confusion and
apathy, whereas meaning generates its own models and motivation and in so
doing frees the student from the teacher. Thus we take charge of our own
learning; there is no other way.

9   Curriculum and community

INTUITION, ANALYSIS AND THE CURRICULUM

I have tried to show how intuition and analysis interactively allow us to construct meaning and create experience of quality. My main theme has been this dialectical relationship, firstly as it is found at the heart of the nature of musical knowledge itself, secondly as it appears in the processes of research, and finally as a necessary tension in education. In this last area I have been specific concerning the implications, both for formal music education in general classes and for specialist instrumental teaching. Our understanding of musical knowing has to be translated, analysed into curriculum planning, a sensitive process during which intuitive insights may too easily be surrendered to educational jargon, the clutter of curriculum writing or the whims of politicians and administrators. I have suggested ways of thinking about music teaching that might avoid inappropriate mechanisation of curriculum practice.

Three layers of musical knowledge – materials, expression, form – have been shown to be points of departure for curriculum activity and a fourth – that of value – can be seen as an ultimate educational aim. It is important to bear in mind that these layers, though logically and analytically distinguishable, are psychologically and intuitively fused together. Outside formal education – in situations of encounter rather than instruction – we may rarely choose to detach ourselves from the on-going sweep of musical engagement to pick apart the layers of meaning that constitute the totality of the experience, knowing that if we do we are liable to sacrifice the integrity of musical response. But in education it is necessary to develop an analytical framework that will help us to order our work. Even so, unless teachers are able to bring to any curriculum structure their own intuitive understanding of both music and the minds of students, 'education' is doomed to sterility.

The teacher of music has always to be a sensitive music critic as well as a good musical model, and although the layers of musical understanding might suggest how we could begin to organise and assess in music education, in the end the quality of models and critics is what really counts. With this cautionary proviso in mind, I can now sketch out an analytical framework for the music curriculum.

Student activities and learning outcomes are the two essential dimensions of all curriculum planning. When organising musical activities and assessing the work of students we should picture the interaction of musical actions and learning outcomes in two interactive dimensions. This avoids confusion and reminds us that activities and learning – though interdependent – are conceptually distinct.

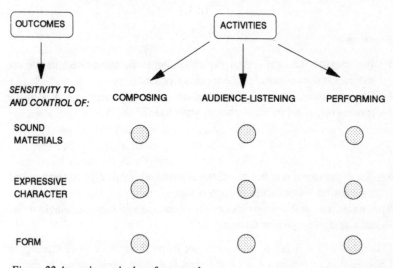

Figure 22 A music curriculum framework

In the matrix (Figure 22), the small circles show the points of intersection between activities and learning. It must be said that composing, performing and audience-listening are to be thought of as those activities at any level through which music is known; the terms do not necessarily imply writing symphonies, giving recitals, going to concerts. As we have already seen, it is possible to start with any of the three activities, to move freely across the matrix and to focus work initially in any of the outcome layers, depending on where students have been before.

We can see the way in which the evaluation of curriculum activities and the assessment of students' work are interlinked. The following sequence of simple questions can be seen as cumulative; for example, if the second can be answered in the affirmative then it becomes possible meaningfully to ask the third or fourth. The process is also cyclic; these questions recur with each project, every activity, whichever particular set of sound materials seems most appropriate.

Materials

1   Is there enjoyment when listening to and exploring the sound qualities of instruments or voices?
2   Is there control in handling instruments or voices and an ability to distinguish between different instruments and ensembles?

Expression

3   Is dramatic gesture, mood or atmosphere communicated in music-making and recognised in the music of others?
4   Are expressive ideas identified and used in conventional ways within a framework of established musical processes?

Form

5   Are expressive ideas perceived and organised effectively in repeating and contrasting relationships to each other?
6   Are musical relationships coherently organised within recognisable styles and can these styles be distinguished?

This piece of curriculum analysis is not to be thought of as consisting of self-contained segments but as representing those major areas in which musical activities are organised. Wherever musical knowing is taking place, we can ask what kind and level of materials are being given attention – perhaps a set of pitched sounds such as a pentatonic scale, the contrast of soft and loud or a chord sequence; and through which particular activities these sets are being explored and mapped. Performing and composing are best related to audience-listening, as those musical processes coming under the control of children are also discovered in the music of someone else. We have already seen that one activity can enhance and promote another and it is better to think of very specific relationships between different musical activities rather than in the metaphor of 'balance' – a term which too easily suggests evenly distributed proportions rather than meaningful integration. Are there opportunities to encounter and analyse the same materials when composing and performing as well as through audience-listening? Are these sounds used

and perceived expressively and woven into engaging structures? Propositional knowledge, knowledge *about* music finds its place discretely and
helpfully alongside these direct understandings; otherwise it can so easily
become a substitute both for intuitive experience and insightful analysis. As
it takes its rightful subordinate place, factual knowledge may illuminate and
enhance musical experience, as it does when we watch Indian dance; it can
be important to know that Krishna played the flute and what certain specific
gestures have come to signify. This kind of information – closely related to
the performance itself – can be important and necessary, though it is never
sufficient.

Beyond these parameters lie deep consequences, the values of personal
and social enrichment that flow from musical engagement, the hidden
curriculum, the reason why we bother with music at all. Music education has
a single main aim: opening up the windows of *value*. It is possible to promote
this aim only by understanding something of the nature of musical knowledge, at least intuitively. Musical value arises from the other knowledge
strands, those of materials, expressive character and structure. In valuing,
knowledge of music is at its most subjective and idiosyncratic, where fusion
between intuition and analysis takes place, a strong sense of the significant
that makes music such a powerful element in every culture. This sense of
value, of commitment, coincides and emerges with other developments that
so often characterise the mid-teens: fervent religious belief, zealous political
affiliation, intense personal relationships and ardent hero-worship. Music is
especially likely to be caught up in these value worlds; it is, after all, a
powerful activity of vital importance in all cultures. Educators are always on
the look-out for the growth of valuing, even if it seems unpredictable, beyond
the reach of day-to-day curriculum planning and classroom practice. This
subjective, personal value knowledge is intertwined with the intuitive and
analytical apprehension of materials, expressive character and form in musical performances. Unless we comprehend something of what is happening
in the layers of musical knowledge there can be only prejudice. But it is
perfectly possible to understand music and still not find value, to play a Bach
Sarabande quite expressively but find it quite boring, to hear *In the South* as
'active' and 'varied' but still not think it 'good'.

The ultimate educational ambition remains the same – that music comes
increasingly to be seen by students as a significant symbolic form. This is the
ultimate heart of musical knowing, opening up the possibility of important
changes of disposition and attitude that may significantly affect our lives,
like the day we fell in love with someone. We 'knew' that it was love; we
came to know 'what's what' in the sense of what was valuable, at least for
us. This is not the same as being told about the delights of love or reading a
record sleeve about a piece of music by Mozart or Paul Simon but rather of

experiencing it ourselves; that expressive and structural elements relate to the way we feel and think and lead us on into new realms of understanding. This attitude cannot be taught – only learned, and it may be that formal structures of education can become an inappropriate context for such personal knowledge.

Fortunately, we are not dependent only on schools and colleges for the growth of musical knowing. Schooling is not the only agent of education; and music is 'out there' in the world beyond the classroom or studio. On this issue of the relationship of music in education and music in society, three of the most influential music educators seem divided. Kodály wanted to initiate children into 'high' culture. Orff seems to create a separate culture of classroom music with special classroom instruments, a children's community where we return to the 'elemental'. But any suggestion of a separate musical world for classrooms would certainly have been resisted by Dalcroze.

> Before everything else, always make sure that the teaching of music is worthwhile. And there must be no confusion as to what is understood by 'music'. There are not two classes of music: one for adults, drawing rooms, and concert halls, the other for children and schools. There is only one music, and the teaching of it is not so difficult a matter as scholastic authorities are apt to suggest at their congresses.
>
> (Jacques-Dalcroze 1967: 93, first published in 1915)

Exactly: education ought not to be a closed system but a facilitative enterprise that draws attention to ideas and processes that exist in the wider world beyond. The preparation of music teachers in college has to reflect this. In a longitudinal study, Edward Gifford alarmingly reveals that limited gains in music and teaching skills acquired during initial primary teacher training seem to be offset by a loss of sense of musical value and enjoyment. Institutional analysis seems to have produced a loss of intuitive response. He concludes:

> It is not a new music curriculum that is being advocated here but a music education which responds to both sides of the dialectic; one where *instruction* and *encounter* both have important roles. Institutionalized education cannot escape the pressures that behavioural objectives place upon instruction and this may be advantageous in shifting the focus of teachers towards the behaviour of students and the detail of the activity. However, learning through a pre-determined sequence of fixed objectives may limit the occurrence of possible encounters during which students will respond in their own way and frame learning experiences for themselves.
>
> (Gifford 1993: 45)

Although curriculum structures are powerful notations which can condition teaching and learning transactions, they are not isolated elements of professional context in which educators work. All professional practice is based on theories of some kind, or at least on hidden assumptions – undeclared theories. Curriculum thinking is also shaped by levels of available technology – in music, the development of mechanisms for producing and transmitting sound. Along with wider theories of social meaning, technology radically extends vocal and instrumental potential and therefore alters our perception of what counts as music and music education, playing a part in shaping what takes place in classrooms and studios.

CHANGING TECHNOLOGY – SERVANT OR MASTER?

Cutting the first gramophone record in 1887 was a significant event in the growth and dissemination of musical discourse, eventually bringing about a dramatic extension of individual choice, access for all to any kind of music, available when and as frequently as anyone might wish. That year saw the first opening of doors to all the musics of the world, both historically and inter-culturally. In the historical sense, we can now recall music stretching back to earlier centuries, thanks to such performers as the Dolmetsch family, Munrow, Harnoncourt and Hogwood. Progressively more available and sophisticated recording techniques have generated a tremendous potential for the development of popular musics, the dissemination of music from every conceivable ethnic and geographical background. We can whistle up Monteverdi, Sting or Miles Davis whenever we like. The implications of increased personal access to music from the ends of the earth and over historical time are still not yet fully comprehended by music educators.

Musical development and cultural revitalisation are dependent on available technical resources and all those related processes that are transmitted within and between musical traditions. The materials of music undergo substantial shifts from place to place and time to time. Music improvised on a xylophone or thumb piano is frequently more angular and spiky in its expressive character than vocal music. These are musical differences that have little to do with social meaning in any extra-musical sense and everything to do with what comes naturally to the hands or breath of the player or easily in singing (Blacking 1976: 12). As we found in our studies of children composing, the sound, shape and layout of instruments is very suggestive of musical possibilities. Musical practices and traditions grow out of the technology of sound materials. Indeed, it might be said that the introduction of what are called 'Orff' instruments into school music classrooms has created classroom musical subcultures, complete with decorative *glissandi* and circling *ostinati*.

Unfortunately – and perhaps because of a misunderstanding of what Orff was about – while aware of the need to simultaneously occupy every child in a class in an 'active' way, it sometimes turned out that everyone played something, often at the same time, no matter how insensitive the result and how trivial the occupation of many of the participants. We were perhaps too ready to assume that an active child is a learning child and had forgotten that much depends on the outcomes of an activity in terms of musical knowledge – whether it is *quality* experience or not. Meanwhile, and outside school, music had become variously experimental, minimalist, pop and rock, while inside some school classrooms the musical subculture often seemed to be based on the materials of pentatonic scales and sounded nothing like music anywhere else in the world, let alone in the students' lives.

By the last decade of the twentieth century the extension of instrumental resources through micro-technology had the effect of opening up classrooms to the same range of instrumental possibilities that are found in the recording studio, the disco and the contemporary concert hall. We can roughly divide up the contribution of the recent evolution of micro-technology into three broad areas. One obvious development is the extension of what used to be called 'programmed instruction' where the potential for independent learning is obviously great. The second area of development is already obvious. There is enough equipment about in daily use to extend instrumental resources in a radical way, giving access to instant accompaniments, quite new tonal effects and undreamed of combinations of sounds able to be controlled both in and out of real time. The third and related area is the development of computers that assist the processes of musical composition.

Any kind of instrumental technology is both a tool and a symbolic prompt, not an end in itself. We all know what happens when we start to really listen to the hi-fi system, rather than through the system to the music. Micro-technology extends the range of musical possibilities, often at the vernacular level, but at the risk of mechanising expressiveness by the use of harmonic and melodic loops and drum patterns, which do not serve the musical imperative of deviation from fixed pulse and mathematically divided rhythms. There are other possibilities, particularly when the computer is used to stimulate compositional processes and to translate visual metaphors of music into sound, as does the computer Xenakis.

If technology can be used to increase the possibility of reaching the required 10 percent of inspiration, leaving most of the 90 percent of perspiration to machinery, then that is certainly an advance. In particular, musical notation is a chore that may be minimised or even made irrelevant by the micro-chip. The authenticity of 'grown up' sound materials is abundantly to hand – especially for young people – without the toil of years of sequential skill practice and drill. Music can be composed and assembled in little bits and layered together without the risk and high-level sensory–motor skills of earlier times – instant control of the vocabulary of the vernacular, but to some extent pre-analysed, not necessarily passing through the selective and creative processes of intuition.

As with the vernacular layer in general, there is a risk that machine-assembled performances will tend towards length, blandness and interchangeability – the technique of scissors and paste; the fate of a good deal of prose-writing under the influence of the word-processor. In spite of many genuinely musical possibilities, we can find computer programs devised along the lines of the old programmed instruction techniques, where either students play notational games that only marginally relate to music, or plod through some fairly well-structured, but ultimately dull sequence of instruction, that may be historically factual in emphasis, or they learn the 'rudiments of music' outside the context of music-making. Back in 1985 an article in a national newspaper drew attention to the various possibilities opening up for music education thanks to computers, the writer concluding that 'musical literacy can now be seen to be within easy reach of young and old alike'. Whatever 'literacy' (notation reading) means divorced from being musically articulate I cannot imagine.

Where micro-technology is especially powerful is in the possibility of giving greater autonomy to each student. The possibility of individualised instruction or small group work without disturbing others is now a reality and headphones help to create private worlds in which it becomes possible for students to make music without coarsening the ears of others. But before we move towards further division of classrooms into separate booths we would be wise to look at the fate of many language laboratories, how often they stand empty, even if in working order. In 'musicing' as in 'languaging' there is an imperative for face-to-face interaction, where people can see, hear and respond to one another. Information technology extends and amplifies the possibilities of making direct musical impact; it gives us decent bass-lines, sets of chords, a vast spectrum of tonal colour, the possibility of shaping ideas directly. It may be that technological progress releases teachers from a fair amount of drudgery – and let us hope students too – leaving us free to use time for other purposes, creating lively *events* in which people can share in musical discourse convivially. Music is a social art.

CULTURAL SIGNALS AND MUSICAL VALUE

Music can be tightly identified with particular cultural groups and their value systems, linked with level of income, religion, dress, ethnic and national origin and general life-style. These elements make their mark on music education and lay behind the political reaction in England, when it seemed to some that the balance of musical examples in the proposed curriculum over-emphasised pop and non-western music at the expense of western classical traditions. Although this interpretation happened to be mistaken, editorials, letters to newspapers and substantial items on radio and TV took up the theme and an unproductive polarisation forced the issue into a caricature; for or against the value of the inherited 'masterworks' as against the ephemeral and subversive nature of pop and 'ethnic' music. Music educators, so the allegation ran, had neglected 'good' knowledge, that of western classical music, and this needed to be redressed.

The question of what counts as 'worthwhile' music lies behind these ideological skirmishes. For it is true that not all knowledge is of equal worth; for example, though there may be a great deal of skill and understanding involved, there is doubtful value in knowing how to torture people, how always to get our own way, how to exploit others for personal gain. There is legitimate or 'quality' knowledge and there is also trivial and negative knowledge. Music, literature, drama and the visual arts are more problematic in this way than science or maths, for although there are important scientific issues such as nuclear energy or ecology that go well beyond school class-rooms, they do not impose themselves so frontally on the educational transaction as do the arts. Students are not usually so committed or opposed to particular views of a mathematical problem or a scientific process as they appear to be in their views of what really counts in music or literature. These areas present educators with awkward choices of selection and presentation; deciding what knowledge is worthwhile is certainly problematic.

This issue has been addressed from a sociological perspective by those who believe that the 'African-American' music (jazz, pop, rock) and other non-western musics have been undervalued by those whose education hap-pens to have initiated them into the western classical traditions – I use the plural 'traditions' deliberately (Swanwick 1968). It has been suggested that when teachers and musicians – seeing the world from the traditions of 'art music' – turn their attention to music originating in other cultures, they tend to misunderstand it and – even if sympathetic – interpret and judge it by the wrong criteria, through the distorting lens of an inappropriate set of critical standards and notation-based analytical techniques (Vulliamy and Lee 1976, Vulliamy 1978, Vulliamy 1980). Shepherd and Vulliamy (1983) have devel-oped a complex theoretical structure which often centres on the issue of staff notation as a particular and limiting slice of musical analysis. Essentially, it is argued that music tends to be judged by criteria directly derived from a system of notation which shapes the musical perception of 'high culture' musicians and educators alike (Shepherd and Vulliamy 1983: 5). They maintain that the improvisatory processes of other musics are devalued in terms of these criteria, drawn from an analytic tradition where the musical materials of pitch and metrical rhythm come to be frozen on the page, 'and so become subject to the total control of the scribehood' (p.13).

If the impersonal filtering of notation prevents students from putting themselves fully into their musical acts, then it also prevents them from fulfilling all aspects of their humanity (p.14).

It could certainly be argued that traditional notation can be an impediment to lively music-making, whatever the style or social context of the music, and that the professional training of musicians and teachers has cultivated the eye and certain types of paper and pencil 'analysis' at the expense of oral fluency and aural sensitivity. We have already seen this tendency in instrumental teaching and it has been noticed by those working within the western traditions (Pratt 1990). In schools and higher education, the more intuitive side of musical understanding can easily be seen as less respectable than analysis by the fixed points of notational precision and the charge of such music being ephemeral may be brought.

> Any domination of popular and temporary cultural movements in our approach to the curriculum will only serve to separate our children from their inheritance which has shaped society today.
>
> (Pascall 1992: 8)

This pronouncement by the then Chairman of the National Curriculum Council was inevitably tied up with a view of artistic knowledge being in good measure propositional knowledge, knowing 'that', and collecting information about the arts can be mere cultural tokenism. It can also lead to a very selective cross-section of what counts as worthwhile music with firm boundaries for inclusion and exclusion.

> An important role of education should be to ensure that every child growing up in Britain, irrespective of their religion or the community in which they live, is taught *about* key traditions and influences within this heritage.
>
> (Pascall 1992: 5, my emphasis)

The idea of the arts as a cultural heritage into which children have to be initiated is not necessarily pernicious but it does need watching. The Third Reich in Germany was in many ways rooted in European high culture and its leaders were certainly very conscious of the importance of the concept of heritage. As Blacking warns, in education the arts should not be used to reinforce tribal boundaries, for views of the arts 'as sensuous gratifications of totemic identities are inevitably corrupting' (Blacking 1987: 147).

Particular musical idioms cannot be vindicated in school and college programmes just by asserting that different criteria apply. Nor ought we to contest the relative values of musical styles, by showing how certain music embodies culturally specific values, the beliefs of a 'tribe'. This same form of argument has been made both for and against the curriculum centrality of the western classical tradition, asserting that some quality of especial cultural value is transmitted, thus reifying a musical genre. It is certainly reasonable to recognise the social nature of all music but to say with Vulliamy that the 'significance of all music is ultimately and inherently social' (Vulliamy 1978: 117), is to overlook the psychological style of the individual partici- pant, specific musical ideas arising from within and travelling across musical traditions, and the available skills and instrumental technology that to some extent determine what is possible in music.

Musical knowledge – while obviously arising in a social context – cannot be permanently locked into a cultural background. If it were so, then it becomes impossible to see how anyone could ever respond to the music of other cultures or other times in any meaningful way. Because of its power as a form of discourse, music is to some extent able to travel across time and between cultures. To this extent it has a degree of symbolic autonomy and is able to be reinterpreted wherever it lands and by whoever finds it.

It is certainly possible to find examples where music is culturally strongly functional at a local level – as in the old African rite of *Candomblé* found in Bahia, Brazil. Music tightly bound into any ritual is very difficult to prise away from its cultural origins for educational or other purposes. We can notice 'that' *Candomblé* involves certain musical procedures, especially particular ways of drumming, but our knowledge 'of' *Candomblé* has to be by participation in the totality of the ritual. My own experience of *Candomblé* suggests that the very presence of 'outsiders' changes the whole focus of the activity. On one occasion at which I was present, the intended trance-like state of the female participants was badly compromised by their family overloading the electrical system to run powerful lights for a video-recorder, causing a total black-out. This attempt to document the event, to analyse and package it for commercial purposes, violated the intuitively social nature of the enterprise.

Here we see the dangers of 'musical fetishism', a concept in part based on the formulation by Marx of 'commodity fetishism', where exchange- value 'usurps the use-value of an object and becomes the means which objects take on and communicate their value' (Green 1988: 86). Fetishism is most obvious in the case of the visual arts, where paintings can be sold at a price calculated on the basis of rarity rather than for any intrinsic value as works of art. The same tendency is also apparent in music, when the marketing of particular performers is based on appeals to social status, age or cultural group. Cash benefit and artistic value may sometimes be inter- twined but they are not synonymous. But fetishism is not to be confused with esteeming music for the perceived contribution it makes to the life of an individual or a community. There are indeed accumulations of valued cultural meaning passed on between generations but music is not just an empty vehicle waiting to be filled up for such cultural transportation but a symbolic abstraction, an analysis of the particular into a more shareable universal form. Music is an active, shaping agent of meaning, not a passive carrier.

What then are these 'meanings' that music embodies? Meyer develops his influential theory of music primarily in terms of what Green refers to as 'inherent musical meaning'; meaning arising in response to musical structure, our response to repetition and change framed by our psychological expectations of musical future based on our experience of musical past (Meyer 1956). This can be set against the idea of 'delineated musical meaning', a range of significance arising from personal association and the social context in which music is perceived and to which it may seem to refer. These meanings relate to the strands of musical experience as I have attempted to define them, though the relationship is not categorical. Expressive character may encompass social references and specific associations, though it more often consists in undesignated abstractions of movement, weight and size. All response to music necessarily includes both delineated and inherent meaning but it is particularly in the layer of expressive characterisation that the universe of meanings arising from sound materials and musical form is interlaced with external references, allusions which can be fairly explicit – especially in song, or abstracted as the dynamic properties of feeling – without discernible represented objects, events or situational causes.

It is not possible to separate 'delineated meanings' from the particularity of pieces and performances. Unless any musical performance is coherent as a symbolic occurrence, its role as *music* in any culture is limited to being a sonorous background to other events. Cultural differences are a reality and that they inflect musical procedures is not in dispute. But any claim that music only articulates particular social realities and that its ultimate meaning and value necessarily reside permanently in these social referents, would lead us into such cultural relativism that it would be impossible to conceive how anyone could ever extend the range of music to which they might respond and in which they might meaningfully participate. Strong social references in music may make it impenetrable to an outsider, a network of expressive meanings inaudible if not intolerable to the non-initiate, as happens with the 'in' words and accompanying gestures of many pop songs, or the arch sentimentality and evocation of 'gracious living' of some Viennese waltzes. But it is not necessary to take such a restrictive view of cultural ownership and it is certainly not the way to construe music education.

Music from any cultural origin may have a part to play in any curriculum, not primarily as the release of inhibitions – a function for which schools are ill-adapted – but to gain insights; not to provoke a reaction but to encourage a response; not as a signal for socially controlled behaviour but as a symbol of human achievement and aspiration, whatever the original cultural setting; not simply as an intuitive response to a particular environment but with the element of analysis that characterises the artistic. Music does more than remind us of and reinforce our own local cultural values – though that itself is important; it takes us outside ourselves and enlarges our range. In the context of the school curriculum, music can help to reinforce the identities of minority as well as majority cultural groups; it can help develop a sense of sharing across cultures; above all, it is an initiation into symbolic discourse. Music-making and music-taking are universals of human culture, 'which revolve most often around reciprocal exchange through symbolic, affiliative and economic systems'.

> The primate series illustrates to an extraordinary degree the emergence of curiosity, play, playfulness, anticipation and, ultimately, the ways of seeking, transforming, representing and using information that characterise the human species.
>
> (Bruner [1972] 1974: 171–2)

There is no need to polarise different types of music. Take this observation from a student aged around 14 on the opening of *Hired Gun* (Chris Rea). Such an analysis goes well beyond simply accepting music as a social signal.[1]

> It was quite slow, deep, mysterious, because of the speed. It had small chords, and a melody running over the top; nice and peaceful music, the notes were long and held a lot.

And speaking again about the start of Phil Collins' *That's Just the Way It Is*:

> It had a strong continuous rhythm which continued and repeated, and it was after two bars another tune came up and it sounded quite sad and sleepy, and very slow. There were four beats, low notes and in the middle it had quite different kind of percussion rhythm and had high notes. It is quite moving, and a kind of music that expresses your feelings.

She approaches the start of the *Introduction and Allegro for Strings* (Elgar) in the same spirit, balancing intuition with analysis.

> Very dramatic, very loud and low chords and there were strings playing over the top, and playing down the scale (minor scale). It started very high and shrill, all very loud and then they went down. Then there was a short gap, and it carried on going down lower. Then they started again in a different key and higher and it went down all in chords and it was quite slow and very dramatic.

There is no evidence of any direct cultural reference here, no form of signalling, waving flags, expressing group identity. National anthems, football songs and pop songs may – under certain conditions – serve this social purpose. But musical experience can also be a form of symbolic transaction, characterised by the facility of combination and regeneration, creating fresh meaning through new juxtapositions. Signalling is a way of pointing to things or pointing things up; our social identity, cultural belonging, attitudes to others. This has severe limitations in terms of giving us access to the world of ideas. Technology has played its part in releasing us from the constraints of one time and place.

Any form of expressive reference within music – dramatic, programmatic, biographical, social – is essentially a re-working of these experiences and ideas, a process of *symbolic abstraction,* metaphors which become meaningful through shared use and musically internal cross-references. If this is what is meant by those who advocate any particular form of 'cultural heritage', then all is well. Cultural meanings are indeed woven into the tapestry of all music and we can choose to use or perceive any music as cultural signalling and little more. However, the specific cultural origins of music are not usually its only or final destination and they are always peripheral in musical and therefore in educational transactions. In symbolic discourse, inherent and delineated meanings are held in a creative tension; as Lucy Green says, in a relationship that is dialectical, not dualistic.

Sharing in this universal dialectical process, the evolution of human societies can also be seen to play out the developmental pattern of individual growth in an analogous way; what Jürgen Habermas calls 'homologies' (Habermas 1976: 104). Following Piaget, in seeking the 'developmental logic behind the process in which structures are formed' (p.169), Habermas characterises the limited representational mode of very early communities as 'particularistic and not very coherent'; we might say rooted in the immediate, the directly sensory, lacking steady images, the equivalent of the musical sensory/manipulative layer. The arrival of reliable mental images – metaphorical thinking – heralded a change making possible 'the construction of a complex of analogies in which all natural and social phenomena were interwoven and could be transformed into one another': the age of mythology. Narrative then becomes possible; absent objects and events can be brought to mind, stories can be told. Parallels to music's expressiveness can thus be seen emerging in all forms of discourse, including the definition and depiction of social order, of law-making.

Then comes a transformation from merely mythological thinking and more tightly argued cosmic views emerge, especially in the great religions of the world – 'teachable knowledge that can be dogmatised' (p.105). Can this be seen as the 'speculative' and 'idiomatic' played out within a larger frame of reference; the search for coherent and socially shared structures? And growing from this authoritarian representational mode emerge modern 'world interpretations' tending to depend more on the search for 'theoretical and practical reason', asserting and testing out world-views more reflectively, giving and listening to reasons and perspectives, becoming aware of competing value systems; more symbolic than signalling, an awareness of the complexities of competing value systems.

What Habermas sees as 'the evolutionary learning mechanism' has in common with its biological analogy the process of mutation, where divergencies are produced that may in time become important for the survival and development of any species. Nature is not into cloning. Small variations occur which change the reaction potential of individual organisms and these mutations may become developmentally significant. Transposed to the social level, this same imperative seems to hold, though in a different way.

> In the case of social evolution the learning process takes place not through changes in genetic makeup but through changes in knowledge potential.
>
> (Habermas 1976: 171)

Fortunately, parents cannot culturally mould their children any more than they are able to clone them genetically; nor can any social order entirely shape the thinking of its members. The so-called 'generation gap' is an essential condition for human flexibility and this 'gap' – this margin of manoeuvre – is kept open by systems of discourse which facilitate the growth of knowledge for any individual and through individuals to society: objectification of our intuitive understanding of the world.

Though symbolic production is not always earth-moving in its consequences – the process of mutation being naturally somewhat wasteful – it sometimes engenders results which, though they may at first be contrary to local conventional commonsense, eventually become part of the intellectual heritage. Presumably these are the 'great' works, dependent for their existence on the vast abundance of the simply 'good', from which their artistic vocabulary is drawn and through which some of the rules of symbolic discourse are developed and shared.

Whatever the cosmic implications of such meta-theorising, a study of musical knowing clearly has implications well beyond the musically specific. Among the other arts, music is a prime instance of the traffic of ideas up and down the modes of representation. Its power consists in being multi-level, engaging us from the particularity of the sensory, through expressive metaphors to the relationships of structured argument. At any of these levels, the interaction of intuition and analysis – of aesthetic enjoyment and artistic traditions – is potentially rich in bringing about what Habermas calls 'divergent phenotypes' (p.170); witness the richness and range of musical idioms and the multitude of distinctive individual musical voices. As a phenomenon, such highly developed symbolic discourse is manifestly part of the developmental thrust of human-kind and worth attention if only for that reason.

In this book I have tried to show how musical discourse is configured: in layers that encompass the domain of 'sound' itself as direct physical sensation; the metaphors of expressive gestures embodied in pitch, rhythm, loudness and timbre shifts, which can communicate something of other times and places, as well as affirm what we already know from our own cultural setting; the capacity to engage us in exploring, anticipating and following structural change, new ways of construing the world. Our attention should focus on musical processes and shared meanings rather than socio-cultural contexts – which usually amount to knowing about rather than knowledge of. In education this will be achieved largely through practical work, not only through performance in bands and choirs but in the more open situation of musical encounters, of small group and individual decisions, when performing and composing give intuitive knowing some space to flower and alternative modes of analysis some scope for growth.

The musical processes that constitute the substance of such activities will be identified and located within a whole range of cultures, not least in the richly developed traditions of the western classical heritage. Unless we get this right, music education is likely to drift off course. Though we can guarantee nothing, music encountered in this way is more likely to be felt as valuable and not perceived as a mere goodwill gesture, cultural tokenism or as a diversion from the 'serious' business of a curriculum. It may then be felt as *quality*. I end as I began, with a description of music.[2]

> Paul Chambers playing bass leads off, low C gently falling to G. Then Davis – trumpet muted – echoes the falling fifth, playing D drifting down to G, thus beginning the first solo of *Flamenco Sketches*. As we listen we move through five serene unfoldings of something that seems to approximate a twelve-bar blues sequence. At least the structural expectations of the blues form are aroused, especially the slightly greater expressive reach of the second line and the gathering of melodic and harmonic strangeness in the third. It is here in this third line that the arabic Andalusian world of *flamenco* is invoked; the set of notes runs D, E♭ (E), F, G, (A) and down again, variously transposed. The penultimate verse – Bill Evans on piano – is the leanest, spare in texture with many single star-like notes picked out before the modal final line returns.

What then, is this music really about and if there is any meaning, as Hesse says, does it really 'need my explanations'? It is 'about' sound materials, especially the Phrygian mode falling characteristically to its tonic by a half-tone, embodied in a chorus returning at the end of each solo over gently sketched textures; it is about a certain way of feeling; it embodies a particular view of the world, that of Miles Davis and the other musicians; it is about the idioms of jazz, blues and echoes of *flamenco,* their potential relationships and our expectations of change and affirmation; it is about the commitment of musicians to music as a powerful form of discourse, able to transcend time and place and the limitations of any single human mind. It is about what Robert Pirsig calls 'quality' and musical experience can indeed be quality; for the concept of quality contains within it the sense of freedom that we find in this margin of manoeuvre.

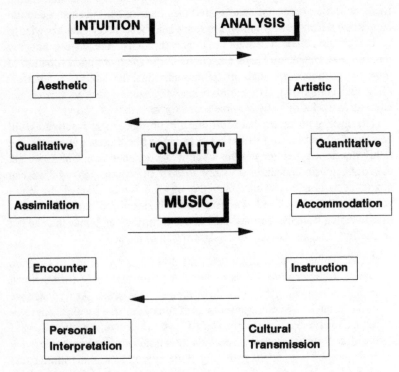

Figure 23 'Quality', music and education

Ultimately, all 'meaning', all 'knowledge' is a personal, individual interpretation of life experience: there is no such thing experientially as neutral data. Each one of us sails and charts the course of our own floating Ark. Life gains significance and shape in musical events, where intuition and analysis meet and where meaning is both celebrated and created. As in all forms of symbolic discourse, music has the potential to take us beyond ourselves, our own small space in time and our local tribe; extending knowledge, enlarging mind, keeping open our capacity for knowing.

We have to be reasonably sure that formal education and teaching is framed and conducted in ways that are compatible with this aspiration; otherwise we should leave well alone.

Notes

INTRODUCTION

1   My reluctance to engage in a method either of detached philosophical speculation
    or myopic empiricism has some support in what has been called Critical Theory,
    a movement represented especially by the work of Adorno, Dilthey, Pollock and
    Habermas (Connerton 1976).

CHAPTER 1

1   It is not my intention to directly engage with many of the writers whose work
    might seem to relate to this deliberately 'unscholarly' analysis. The concepts of
    materials, expression and form turn up frequently in the well-known literature on
    aesthetics; for instance in Leonard Meyer, Monroe Beardsley and Ralph Smith.
    Bennett Reimer – for one – has sharply portrayed a division between 'referential-
    ism' and 'formalism' (Reimer 1989). Such a debate seems to me to polarise rather
    than facilitate discussion of the complexity of musical knowing and I have chosen
    to steer clear of this and other philosophical reefs, preferring to run aground in
    my own boat. However, a good initial reference showing the recent state of play
    in the USA is *The Journal of Aesthetic Education*, Vol. 25, No. 3, Fall 1991.
    There are also parallels in linguistic analysis – phonetic theory (materials),
    semantic theory (expression) and syntactic theory (form). Jürgen Habermas gives
    a good overview of this kind of analysis in his essay 'What is Universal
    Pragmatics?' (1976/1984).

CHAPTER 3

1   The semantic differential was brought to light by Osgood *et al.* (1957) but has
    since been extensively employed in various branches of psychological investiga-
    tion. Those employing it in music education include Swanwick (1973), Miller
    (1980), Cox (1989), Madsen and Duke (1985), and Fujihara and Tagashira
    (1984).
2   I am grateful for the help of Graham Conridge, Catherine Foster and Rhona Povey
    for carrying out the work in schools.
3   A Wilcoxon Matched Pairs test shows all changes to be statistically significant
    at p≤0.01, except on the 'Complex' scale (p≤0.05) and for two non-significant

results – the 'Varied' scale between sessions 1 and 3 and 'Good' between sessions 1 and 2. The numbers of 'low' first scores range between 16 and 50 percent of the 71 children, depending on the particular scale. To give the full name, a Wilcoxon Matched Pairs Signed Ranks test assesses the effect of the magnitude between the ranking order of differences between pairs of scores.

4   A Mann-Whitney U-Test gives p≤0.01 for 'Bright' between the low and high starters on the third session and p≤0.05 for 'Good'. This test examines two groups of independent scores to see if the observations differ in central tendency.

5   The distinction between meaning 'to' and 'for' is made in Swanwick (1979). It is possible to find something meaningful in the sense of our knowing what is being said or presented but not to see this as important or necessarily worthwhile for our own lives; it may have little or no significance 'for' us as an individual although we may understand what is being communicated 'to' us. In effect, we may be able to 'read' the sound materials and interpret expressive character and form perfectly well but still fail to find engagement with music lacking in any personal significance.

CHAPTER 5

1   It would be out of character with the general thesis and tone of this book to get into the fine detail of Piaget's work. However, it is possible to find close correspondences between his explicit descriptions and the implications of the developmental spiral. It might be best to conceive of the first three levels of the developmental spiral as matching Piaget's 'sensory–motor activity', 'egocentric representative activity' and 'operational activity'– concepts that are close to Bruner's enactive, iconic and symbolic modes of representation.

2   The resulting data became available thanks to Michael Stavrides, who is the Primary Music Inspector for the island and was then a research student with the writer. I am most grateful to him and other colleagues and teachers in Cyprus for their help and encouragement.

3   Table 1 gives the correlations between seven judges' assignments of compositions by criteria, ranked in ascending order on the spiral and between these assignments and the actual ages of the children. The test here is the Spearman Rank Correlation Coefficient which measures the degree of association in pairs.

Table 1 Correlations between UK judges' criteria ratings and actual age

Judges	1	2	3	4	5	6	7	Age
1	1.00	0.64	0.84	0.77	0.79	0.80	0.72	0.72
2		1.00	0.77	0.68	0.67	0.78	0.73	0.62
3			1.00	0.70	0.82	0.78	0.75	0.70
4				1.00	0.77	0.81	0.76	0.71
5					1.00	0.93	0.84	0.82
6						1.00	0.87	0.84
7							1.00	0.79

N = 28

All levels of significance here are of the order p≤0.001 and the level of concordance between the first seven judges – based on ranking of the ratings in each category – is 0.80, at p≤0.001. We can therefore assume a very high level of agreement between judges and between their estimation and the actual age of the children whose compositions were being evaluated.

4   Table 2 shows the proportion of judgements made on each of the spiral criteria shown against the age levels.

Table 2 Criteria against age levels

	Sens. 1	Man. 2	Pers. 3	Vern. 4	Spec. 5	Idiom. 6	Sym. 7
Age level							
1	12	21	15	1	0	0	0
2	9	11	16	13	0	0	0
3	1	9	8	14	13	4	0
4	0	1	8	4	7	15	14

We would normally expect roughly equal figures in each cell. This is clearly not the case. On 18 degrees of freedom, a X of 145.91 gives an associated probability of $p \le 0.001$, suggesting that age has a great deal to do with the level on which compositions are evaluated.

5   To test for this, the criterion judgements were converted into a set of linear scores by rating each successive level a point higher than the previous one. This permits a rough and ready comparison between the British and Cyprus data. An analysis of variance gives no significant result for the 4/5-year-olds but is statistically significant for both the age groups 7/8 and 10/11, in each case with a probability of $p \le 0.001$. A Mann-Whitney test gives no significant result for differences between the 4/5 years age groups but there is a significant difference between the two populations aged 7/8 (U = 1512.5, $p \le 0.001$) and 10/11 (U = 3601.5, $p \le 0.01$).

CHAPTER 6

1   The General Certificate of Secondary Education is a examination taken throughout schools in England and Wales at the age of 16-plus, consisting of a range of subjects within which music is an option. The examination is run by area boards independent of individual schools, though teachers are involved in assessment.

2   The following table gives this predicted order of the cards and the ranking by the nine groups.

Table 3

ORDER	G1	G2	G3	G4	G5	G6	G7	G8	G9
1	1	3	1	1	1	2	1	1	1
2	2	2	3	2	2	1	3	3	2
3	3	1	2	3	3	3	2	2	3
4	4	4	4	4	4	4	4	4	4
5	5	6	5	5	5	5	5	5	5
6	6	5	6	6	6	6	6	6	6
7	7	7	7	7	7	7	7	7	7
8	8	8	8	8	8	8	8	8	8

The second group is least in line with the predicted order and with the other groups. They also finished the task in the shortest time and indicated that they did not feel the need to discuss and reflect to the same extent as the others. There is also more general disagreement about the relative placing of the second and third cards. Even so, the level of agreement is very high, statistically significantly so. An analysis by the Kendell Coefficient of Concordance gives a 'W' of 0.964, significant at p≤0.0001 and correlations between the nine groups and the predicted card order do not fall below 0.88 and are mostly of 0.97 and upwards. This test determines the extent of agreement among several variables, in this case the views of several judges. A Spearman Correlation Coefficient shows all interrelationships significant at p≤0.001.

3 *Table 4* Correlations between seven performance judges and a GCSE assessor

Judges	1	2	3	4	5	6	GCSE Ex.	
1	1.00	0.68	0.81	0.88	0.89	0.91	0.87	0.76
2		1.00	*0.60	*0.62	0.82	0.73	0.82	*0.60
3			1.00	0.85	0.82	0.89	0.86	0.74
4				1.00	0.89	0.89	0.84	†0.58
5					1.00	0.90	0.85	*0.60
6						1.00	0.94	*0.70
7							1.00	0.77
GCSE Examiner								1.00

Significant at p≤0.01
* = p≤0.5
† = not significant
A Kendall Concordance test gives W = 0.52; (p≤0.001)
W = 0.85, (p≤0.001) if the GCSE marker is removed

4 The correlation between individual judges tends to be almost as high as when actual criterion statements were used and the overall concordance test stands at 0.73 (p≤0.001), against 0.80 in the original study, when we were employing criteria. In this case though, all eight points are used whereas the eighth criterion statement, being specific, was not felt to be appropriate for any of the compositions on this tape.

5 This research was carried out by Liane Hentschke in the Music Department of the London Institute of Education and was a replication of work she had previously undertaken with children in Brazil (Hentschke 1993).

6 Chi-square with four degrees of freedom is 231.97, giving an associated probability of p≤0.0001. Distribution of the pattern of musical criticism certainly seems to change over age.

7 *Table 5* Levels of analysis when listening to music: Brazilian and English data

	Age 6 Plus			Age 9 Plus			Age 13 Plus		
Brazil	57	74	0	42	93	0	8	128	0
England	45	135	0	4	167	9	2	92	86
	M	E	F	M	E	F	M	E	F
	Chi Square = 12.04			Chi Square = 56.17			Chi Square = 91.13		
	p≤0.001			p≤0.001			p≤0.001		

M = Materials
E = Expression
F = Form

CHAPTER 7

1   This work was carried out by Mari Shiobara and we are grateful for the help of Colin Pigeon and his staff at Wheatfields School.

2   *Table 6*   Nine judges place 16 compositions from experimental and control groups

	Experimental	Control
Sensory	61	3
Manipulative	12	9
Personal	21	25
Vernacular	27	55
Speculative	42	30
Idiomatic	18	10
Symbolic	18	2

Chi-square = 30.00; $p \leq 0.0001$

CHAPTER 9

1   I am again indebted to Liane Hentschke for these examples of children talking about music.

2   *Flamenco Sketches*, Miles Davis, *Kind of Blue*, *CDCBS 62066*.

Bibliography

Abbs, P. (1989) (ed.) *The Symbolic Order*, London: The Falmer Press.

Arnold, D. (1983) (ed.) *The New Oxford Companion to Music*, Oxford, New York: Oxford University Press.

Barlow, D. H. and Hersen, M. (1984) *Single Case Experimental Designs*, New York: Pergamon Press.

Bartlett, D. L. (1973) 'Effect of repeated listenings on structural discrimination and affective response,' *Journal of Research in Music Education*, 21, 302–17.

Bentley, A. (1966) *Measure of Musical Abilities*, London: Harrap.

Best, D. (1989) 'Feeling and reason in the arts: the rationality of feeling', in P. Abbs (ed.) *The Symbolic Order*, London: The Falmer Press.

Blacking, J. (1984) 'Versus Gradus Novos Ad Parnassum Musicum: Exemplum Africanum', in *Becoming Human Through Music*, the Western Symposium, August, 1984, Connecticut, USA.

Blacking, J. (1976) *How Musical is Man?*, London: Faber.

Blacking, J. (1987) *A Commonsense View of All Music: Reflections on Percy Grainger's Contribution to Ethnomusicology and Music Education*, Cambridge: Cambridge University Press.

Bloom, B. S., Krathwohl, D. R. and Masia, B. B. (1964) *Taxonomy of Educational Objectives, Book 2, Affective Domain*, New York: David McKay Co.

Bradley, I. (1971) 'Repetition as a factor in the development of musical preferences', *Journal of Research in Music Education*, 19, 295–8.

Bronowski, J. (1951) *The Common Sense of Science*, London: Pelican Books, 1960.

Bruner, J. S. (1962, 1979) *On Knowing: Essays for the Left Hand*, Harvard: Belknap.

Bruner, J. S. (1972) *The Relevance of Education*, Harmondsworth: Penguin, 1974.

Bruner, J. S. (1975) 'The ontogenesis of speech acts', *Journal of Child Language*, 2 (1), 1–19.

Bunting, R. (1977) 'The common language of music, music in the secondary school curriculum', *Working Paper 6*, Schools Council, York University.

Bunting, R. (1988) 'Composing music: case studies in the teaching and learning process', *British Journal of Music Education*, 5 (3), 269–310.

Campbell, D. T. and Stanley, J. C. (1963) *Experimental and Quasi-experimental Design for Research*, Chicago: Rand McNally.

Chester, A. (1970) 'Second thoughts on a rock aesthetic: The Band', *New Left Review*, 62.

Cohen, L. and Manion, L. (1980) *Research Methods in Education*, London: Croom Helm.

Cohn, N. cited in Martin, B. (1981) *A Sociology of Contemporary Cultural Change*, Oxford: Basil Blackwell.

Colwell, R. (1992) (ed.) *Handbook of Research on Music Teaching and Learning*, New York: Schirmer Books.

Connerton, P. (1976) (ed.) *Critical Sociology*, Harmondsworth: Penguin.

Cook, N. (1990) *Music, Imagination and Culture*, Oxford: Clarendon Press.

Cox, J. (1989) 'Rehearsal organisational structures used by successful Ohio high school choral directors', *Journal of Research in Music Education*, 37, 201–18.

Croce, B. (1900) *Aesthetic: As Science of Expression and General Linguistic*, London: Peter Owen, 1953/1972.

Curwen, A. J. (1913) *The Teacher's Guide to Mrs. Curwen's Pianoforte Method*, London: Curwen & Sons.

Davies, C. (1992) 'Listen to my song: a study of songs invented by children aged 5 to 7 years', *British Journal of Music Education*, 9 (1), March, 19–48.

Department of Education and Science (1987a) *The National Curriculum 5–16*, London: HMSO.

Department of Education and Science (1987b) *The National Curriculum Task Group on Assessment and Testing – A Report*, London: HMSO.

Department of Education and Science (1991a) *The National Curriculum Music Working Group, Interim Report*, London: HMSO.

Department of Education and Science (1991b) *Music for Ages 5 to 14*, August, London: HMSO.

Department of Education and Science (1992) *Draft Order for Music*, 27 January, London: HMSO.

Dewey, J. (1934) *Art as Experience*, New York: Capricorn Books, 1958.

Eisner, E. (1981) 'On the differences between scientific and artistic approaches to qualitative research, *Educational Researcher*, 10 (4), 5–9.

Eisner, E. W. (1991) *The Enlightened Eye: Qualitative Inquiry and the Enhancement of Educational Practice*, New York: Macmillan.

Fransella, F. and Bannister, D. (1977) *A Manual for Repertory Grid Technique*, London: Academic Press.

Fujihara, T. and Tagashira, N. (1984) 'A multidimensional scaling for classical music perception', *Japanese Journal of Psychology*, 55 (2), 75–9.

Gardner, H. (1973) *The Arts and Human Development*, New York: Wiley.

Gifford, E. (1993) 'The musical training of primary teachers', *British Journal of Music Education*, 10 (1), 34–46.

Gilbert, L. (1990) 'Aesthetic development in music: an experiment in the use of personal construct theory', *British Journal of Music Education*, 7 (3), 173–90.

Green, L. (1988) *Music on Deaf Ears: Musical Meaning, Ideology and Education*, Manchester: Manchester University Press.

Habermas, J. (1976) *Communication and the Evolution of Society*, trans. T. Macarthy, Cambridge: Polity Press, 1991.

Hamlyn, D. W. (1970) *The Theory of Knowledge*, London and New York: Macmillan.

Hanslick, E. (1854) *The Beautiful in Music*, Indianapolis: Bobbs-Merrill, 1957.

Hargreaves, D. J. (1984) 'The effect of repetition on liking for music', *Journal of Research in Music Education*, 32, 35–47.

Hargreaves, D. J. (1986) *The Developmental Psychology of Music*, Avon: Cambridge University Press.

Harvey, A. W. (1986) 'Is brain research relevant for music education?', *British Journal of Music Education*, 3 (2), 175–9.

Heller, J. and Campbell, W. (1985) 'Response: view from the Fourth Estate', *Bulletin of the Council for Research in Music Education*, No. 83, Summer.

Hentschke, L. (1993) 'Musical development: testing a model in the audience-listening setting', Unpublished PhD thesis, University of London Institute of Education.

Hesse, H. (1943) *The Glass Bead Game*, Harmondsworth: Penguin, 1972.

Jacques-Dalcroze, E. (1967) *Rhythm, Music and Education*, trans. H. F. Rubinstein, London: Riverside Press (first published in 1915).

Keetman, G. (1974) *Elementaria: First Acquaintance with Orff-Schulwerk*, London: Schott.

Keil, C. (1966) 'Motion and feeling through music', *Journal of Aesthetics and Art Criticism*, 24, 337–49.

Kelly, G. (1955) *The Psychology of Personal Constructs*, Vols 1 and 2, New York: Norton.

Kivy, P. (1991) 'Music and the liberal education', *Journal of Aesthetic Education*, 25 (3), 79–93.

Klein, A. H. (1963) *Graphic Worlds of Peter Bruegel the Elder*, New York: Dover Publications Inc.

Kodály, Z. (1974) *The Selected Writings of Zoltan Kodály*, London: Boosey & Hawkes.

Kratochwill, T. R. (1978) (ed.) *Single Subject Research: Strategies for Evaluating Change*, Orlando, Florida: Academic Press Inc.

Langer, S. K. (1942) *Philosophy in a New Key*, New York: Mentor Books and Cambridge, MA: Harvard University Press.

Langer, S. K. (1953) *Feeling and Form*, London: Routledge.

Langer, S. K. (1967) *Mind: An Essay on Human Feeling*, Vol. 1, Baltimore: Johns Hopkins Press.

Laurence, Dan H. (ed.) (1981) *Shaw's Music*, London: The Bodley Head.

Leonhard, C. and House, R. W. (1959) *Foundations and Principles of Music Education*, New York: McGraw-Hill.

Loane, B. (1984) 'On "listening" in music education', *British Journal of Music Education*, I (1), 27–36.

Madsen, C. K. and Duke, R. A. (1985) 'Observation of approval/disapproval in music: perceptions versus actual classroom events', *Journal of Research in Music Education*, 33, 205–14.

Manchester Guardian, 15 March, 1904.

MENC (1993) *Soundpost*, 9 (3), 17–30.

Meyer, L. B. (1956) *Emotion and Meaning in Music*, University of Chicago Press, and Chicago and London: University of California Press, 1973.

Meyer, L. B. (1959) 'Some remarks on value and greatness in music', *Journal of Aesthetics and Art Criticism*, Vol. 17.

Miles, M. B. and Huberman, A. M. (1984) 'Drawing meaning from qualitative data: toward a shared craft', *Educational Researcher*, May.

Miller, R. F. (1980) 'An analysis of musical perception through multi-dimensional scaling', Unpublished doctoral dissertation, University of Illinois, Urbana.

Mills, J. (1991) *Music in the Primary School*, Cambridge: Cambridge University Press.

National Curriculum Council (1992) Consultation Report, York, England.

Orff, C. (1964) 'Orff-Schulwerk: past and future', *Music in Education*, Sept/Oct.

Osgood, C. E., Suci, G. J. and Tannenbaum, P. H. (1957) *The Measurement of Meaning*, University of Illinois, Urbana.

Pacey, F. (1993) 'Schema theory and the effect of variable practice in string teaching', *British Journal of Music Education*, 10 (2).

Pascall, D. (1992) 'The cultural dimension in education', *Arts, Culture and Education*, Oxford: National Foundation for the Arts, 4–8.

Paynter, J. (1992) *Sound and Structure*, Cambridge: Cambridge University Press.

Piaget, J. (1951) *Play, Dreams and Imitation in Childhood*, New York: Norton and Co. (Norton Library, 1962).

Pirsig, R. M. (1974) *The Art of Motorcycle Maintenance* (first published in Britain by The Bodley Head), Uxbridge: Corgi, 1976.

Plummeridge, C. (1991) *Music Education in Theory and Practice*, London: The Falmer Press.

Polanyi, M. and Prosch, H. (1975) *Meaning*, Chicago: University of Chicago Press.

Popper, K. (1972) *Objective Knowledge*, Oxford: Clarendon Press.

Pratt, G. (1990) *Aural Awareness: Principles and Practice*, Milton Keynes: Open University Press.

Priest, P. (1989) 'Playing by ear: its nature and application to instrumental learning', *British Journal of Music Education*, 6 (2), 173–91.

Regelski, T. A. (1983) *Teaching General Music: Action Learning for Middle and Secondary Schools*, New York: Schirmer Books.

Regelski, T. A. (1992) *The Action Value of Musical Experience*, in *Companion to Contemporary Musical Thought*, eds Paynter, J., Howell, T., Orton, R. and Seymour, P., London: Routledge, pp. 105–27.

Reid, L. A. (1986) *Ways of Understanding and Education*, Studies in Education 18, University of London Institute of Education, Heinemann.

Reimer, B. (1985) 'Toward a more scientific approach to music education research', *Bulletin of the Council for Research in Music Education*, No. 83, Summer.

Reimer, B. (1989) *A Philosophy of Music Education*, New Jersey: Prentice Hall.

Richards, I. A. (1960) *Principles of Literary Criticism*, London: Routledge.

Russell, B. (1912) *The Problems of Philosophy*, London: Oxford University Press.

Ryle, G. (1949) *The Concept of Mind*, London and New York: Hutchinson, Penguin, 1963.

Schmidt, R. A. (1975) 'A schema theory of discrete motor skill learning', *Psychological Review*, 82 (4), 225–59.

Schools Update 1992 For Teachers and Governors, News from the DFE, NCC and SEAC, Department for Education, England, Summer. 1992.

Seashore, C. E. (1938) *The Psychology of Music*, New York: McGraw Hill.

Shaw, G. B. (1920) *Music and Letters*, January, 1920 and in *Shaw's Music*, ed. Dan H. Laurence, London: The Bodley Head, 1981.

Shepherd, J., Verden, P., Vulliamy, G. and Wishart, T. (1977) *Whose Music? A Sociology of Musical Languages*, London: Transaction Books, reprinted New Brunswick, 1980.

Shepherd, J. and Vulliamy, G. (1983) 'A comparative sociology of school knowledge', *British Journal of Sociology of Education*, 4 (1).

Shiobara, M. (1993) 'The effect of movement on musical comprehension', Unpublished PhD thesis, University of London Institute of Education.

Simpson, K. (1976) *Some Great Music Educators*, London: Novello.

Sloboda, J. A. (1985) *The Musical Mind: The Cognitive Psychology of Music*, Oxford: Oxford University Press.

Sluckin, W., Hargreaves, D. J. and Colman, A. M. (1982) 'Some experimental studies of familiarity and liking', *Bulletin of the British Psychological Society*, 35, 189–94.

Strauss, A. L. (1987) *Qualitative Analysis for Social Scientists*, Cambridge: Cambridge University Press.

Swanwick, K. (1968) *Popular Music and the Teacher*, Oxford: Pergamon Press.

Swanwick, K. (1973) 'Musical cognition and aesthetic response', *Bulletin of the British Psychological Society*, 26, 285–9.

Swanwick, K. (1979) *A Basis for Music Education*, Windsor: NFER-Nelson.

Swanwick, K. (1983) *The Arts in Education: Dreaming or Wide Awake?* A special professorial lecture delivered on 4 November, 1982 and subsequently published in 1983 by the University of London Institute of Education.

Swanwick, K. (1984) 'Problems of sociological approach to pop music in schools', *British Journal of Sociology of Education*, 5, 49–56.

Swanwick, K. (1988) *Music, Mind and Education*, London: Routledge.

Swanwick, K. (1989) 'Music in schools: a study of context and curriculum practice', *British Journal of Music Education*, 6 (4), 155–71.

Swanwick, K. (1992) *Music Education and the National Curriculum*, The London File, University of London Institute of Education, London: Tufnell Press.

Swanwick, K. and Jarvis, C. (1990) *The Tower Hamlets String Teaching Project: A Research Report*, University of London Institute of Education.

Swanwick, K. and Tillman, J. (1986) 'The sequence of musical development: a study of children's composition', *British Journal of Music Education*, 3 (3), November, 305–39.

Taylor, D. (1989) 'Physical movement and memory for music', *British Journal of Music Education*, 6 (3), 251–60.

Thompson, K. (1983) 'An analysis of group instrumental teaching', Unpublished PhD Dissertion, University of London.

Thompson, K. (1984) 'An analysis of group instrumental teaching', *British Journal of Music Education*, 1 (2), 153–71.

Vulliamy, G. (1978) 'Culture clash and school music: a sociological analysis', in L. Barton and R. Meighan (eds), *Sociological Interpretations of Schooling and Classrooms: A Reappraisal*, London: Driffeld.

Vulliamy, G. (1980) 'Music education and music languages', *Australian Journal of Music Education*, April.

Vulliamy, G. and Lee, E. (1976) *Pop Music in School*, Cambridge: Cambridge University Press.

Vulliamy, G. and Shepherd, J. (1984) 'Sociology and music education: a response to Swanwick', *British Journal of Sociology of Education*, 5, 57–76.

Wapnick, J. (1976) 'A review of research on attitude and preference', *Bulletin of the Council for Research in Music Education*, 48, 1–20.

Ward, D. J. (1986) 'Personal construct theory: its application to research in music education', in M. Ross (ed.), *Assessment In Arts Education*, Vol. 6, Oxford: Pergamon Press.

Warnock, M. (1976) *Imagination*, London: Faber.

Yin, R. K. (1989) *Case Study Research, Design and Methods*, London: Sage.

Young, P. (1978) *Playing the String Game*, Austin: University of Texas.

Index